Samuel French Acting Edition

Candle-Light
A Comedy in Three Acts

by
Siegfried Geyer

Adapted by
P.G. Wodehouse

SAMUELFRENCH.COM   SAMUELFRENCH.CO.UK

Copyright © 1927 under title *Kleine Komoedie* by George Marton, Verlag
Copyright © 1929 by Gilbert Miller
Copyright © 1934 by Samuel French
Copyright © 1955 (in Renewal) by Camilla Geyer
Copyright © 1955 (in Renewal) by Pelham Grenville Wodehouse
All Rights Reserved

CANDLE-LIGHT is fully protected under the copyright laws of the United States of America, the British Commonwealth, including Canada, and all other countries of the Copyright Union. All rights, including professional and amateur stage productions, recitation, lecturing, public reading, motion picture, radio broadcasting, television and the rights of translation into foreign languages are strictly reserved.

ISBN 978-0-573-60674-8

www.SamuelFrench.com
www.SamuelFrench.co.uk

For Production Enquiries

United States and Canada
Info@SamuelFrench.com
1-866-598-8449

United Kingdom and Europe
Plays@SamuelFrench.co.uk
020-7255-4302

Each title is subject to availability from Samuel French, depending upon country of performance. Please be aware that *CANDLE-LIGHT* may not be licensed by Samuel French in your territory. Professional and amateur producers should contact the nearest Samuel French office or licensing partner to verify availability.

CAUTION: Professional and amateur producers are hereby warned that *CANDLE-LIGHT* is subject to a licensing fee. Publication of this play(s) does not imply availability for performance. Both amateurs and professionals considering a production are strongly advised to apply to Samuel French before starting rehearsals, advertising, or booking a theatre. A licensing fee must be paid whether the title(s) is presented for charity or gain and whether or not admission is charged. Professional/Stock licensing fees are quoted upon application to Samuel French.

No one shall make any changes in this title(s) for the purpose of production. No part of this book may be reproduced, stored in a retrieval system, or transmitted in any form, by any means, now known or yet to be invented, including mechanical, electronic, photocopying, recording, videotaping, or otherwise, without the prior written permission of the publisher. No one shall upload this title(s), or part of this title(s), to any social media websites.

For all enquiries regarding motion picture, television, and other media rights, please contact Samuel French.

MUSIC USE NOTE

Licensees are solely responsible for obtaining formal written permission from copyright owners to use copyrighted music in the performance of this play and are strongly cautioned to do so. If no such permission is obtained by the licensee, then the licensee must use only original music that the licensee owns and controls. Licensees are solely responsible and liable for all music clearances and shall indemnify the copyright owners of the play(s) and their licensing agent, Samuel French, against any costs, expenses, losses and liabilities arising from the use of music by licensees. Please contact the appropriate music licensing authority in your territory for the rights to any incidental music.

IMPORTANT BILLING AND CREDIT REQUIREMENTS

If you have obtained performance rights to this title, please refer to your licensing agreement for important billing and credit requirements.

CANDLE-LIGHT

STORY OF THE PLAY

A comedy which relates how Prince Rudolf's valet falls in love with a pretty voice over the telephone, invites his charmer to his master's first-floor apartment, and then, naturally, puts off his livery and becomes a Prince—all this is related with an arid, wiry wit that is capital entertainment. Particularly when Prince Rudolf returns unexpectedly in person and sardonically accepts the situation by donning his valet's livery—particularly then are the lines neatly turned and the situations nicely groomed in the acting. Your sympathies are very much with the ambitious valet who confesses that his previous love affairs have been confined to "cooks and maids, with possibly a governess at Christmas." The title is from the old quotation: "Choose neither women nor linen by candle-light."

Copy of program of the first performance of "CANDLE-LIGHT" as produced at The Empire Theatre, New York:

GILBERT MILLER

Presents

Gertrude Lawrence in

"CANDLE-LIGHT"

A Comedy in Three Acts

By SIEGFRIED GEYER

Adapted by P. G. Wodehouse

CHARACTERS

PRINCE RUDOLF HASELDORF-SCHLOBITTEN—	*Reginald Owen*
JOSEF, *his valet*	*Leslie Howard*
BARON VON RISCHENHEIM	*Robert English*
BARONESS VON RISCHENHEIM	*Betty Schuster*
LISERL	*Rita Vale*
MARIE	*Gertrude Lawrence*
A WAITER	*Ralph Roberts*
KOEPPKE, *a chauffeur*	*Jack Carlton*

The action takes place between seven and ten o'clock of an evening in December, in PRINCE RUDOLF'S *apartment.*

TIME: *The Present.*

DESCRIPTION OF CHARACTERS:

MARIE: *A pretty, petite girl—sufficiently refined to pass for a lady—with a fine sense of humor—25.*

PRINCE RUDOLF: *Tall, good-looking, dark—33.*

JOSEF: *Distinguished, polite, charming. Light. 33. Same build as* RUDOLF.

BARON: *A heavily-built, aristocratic man of 40.*

BARONESS: *A dashing, impetuous, beautiful aristocrat. 30.*

LISERL: *A fiery, smartly dressed girl of 27.*

WAITER *and* CHAUFFEUR: *Typical.*

CANDLE-LIGHT

ACT ONE

SCENE: *A small drawing-room in the* PRINCE'S *bachelor apartments, luxuriously but tastefully furnished.*
 Rear Center, double doors to passage and double doors to library. Down R. *front, door to the* PRINCE'S *bedroom. Down* L. *front, door to smoking-room. See scene design.*

TIME: *It is seven o'clock.*

AT RISE OF CURTAIN: *The TELEPHONE is ringing. Enter,* R., JOSEF, *who switches on LIGHTS,* L. *of* C. *doors, and then crosses to telephone. Speaks in suave, dignified voice.*

JOSEF. Hullo? This is Prince Rudolf's valet speaking. *(Pause—sharply)* Who's that? *(With sudden amiability)* Oh, I beg your pardon, your Excellency. *(Bows)* I did not recognize your Excellency's voice. I'm not quite sure, your Excellency. I will inquire immediately—— (PRINCE RUDOLF *appears in* R. *doorway, without coat and vest, his black braces on, one side done up and one hanging loose, and his black tie partly tied. He gesticulates, pantomiming: "Say I'm out."* JOSEF *puts his hand over mouthpiece and turns to* PRINCE. *Reassuring-*

ly) No, your Highness, *not* a lady. It is His Excellency, Count Hoisten.

PRINCE. *(Relieved)* Oh! Tell him I'm coming. *(Advances to down* C.*)*

JOSEF. *(Into phone)* His Highness is on his way, your Excellency. *(Holds phone to* PRINCE'S *ear.)*

PRINCE. *(*C.*)* Hullo. Good evening, Excellency. —What's that? Now? I'm afraid—— Oh, Lord Charles? Yes,—*(Crosses to* C. *armchair and stands in front of it)*—of course I remember him—played polo with him last year. *(Sits,* JOSEF *holding receiver to his ear)* Still, I don't quite see how I can manage. Eh? Oh, well, if he's leaving tomorrow—of course, in that case—where are you meeting him? Very well, I'll come. (JOSEF *is about to replace phone.* PRINCE *calls him back)* I beg your pardon? Oh, no, nothing that can't be put off. I'll be there in half an hour. Goodbye. (JOSEF *replaces phone in box.)* Damn. What tie, Josef? *(Takes off black tie, which* JOSEF *takes.)*

JOSEF. Very good, your Highness. *(Exits* R. PRINCE, *walking round sofa from* L. *to* R. *and back to in front of* C. *chair, puts up braces and* JOSEF *immediately re-enters with tail coat, white waistcoat, a white tie, handkerchief, and a small white cardboard box containing one red and one white carnation. He places box of flowers on table* R.C. PRINCE *takes tie.* JOSEF *places clothes on back of armchair* C. *and handkerchief on arm)* Your Highness is going out?

PRINCE. Yes.

JOSEF. But Fraulein Liserl is due here at seven sharp.

PRINCE. I know. You must telephone and put her off.

JOSEF. Telephone and put her off! Very good, your Highness. *(Short silence. Takes waistcoat off back of chair and shows it)* This waistcoat?

PRINCE. Yes.

JOSEF. *(Pretends to put buttons in waistcoat)* And—what explanation shall I give to Fraulein Liserl?

PRINCE. Say I shan't be here.

JOSEF. Shan't be here. Very good, your Highness.

PRINCE. You looked pained, Josef. You don't think that's a good explanation?

JOSEF. A little curt, perhaps, considering the lady has been with us for nearly two months.

PRINCE. *(Looks at him)* With us! Oh, well, tell her that His Excellency, Count Holsten, called up unexpectedly, and asked me to come and meet an old friend from England.

JOSEF. *(Rather shocked)* But that's the truth!

PRINCE. I know. It can't be helped—for once.

JOSEF. Very good, your Highness. But I fancy women are not very fond of the truth.

PRINCE. What makes you think that?

JOSEF. Oh, well, your Highness, one has had experiences.

PRINCE. *(Tieing tie)* Ah?

JOSEF. *(Deprecatingly)* On quite a modest scale, of course. Nothing pretentious.

PRINCE. But enjoyable?

JOSEF. Oh, extremely. And they all preferred a nice romantic lie.

PRINCE. Well, I suppose there's not much difference between women, whatever their rank in life. *(Squinting down at his clothes)* That seems all right.

JOSEF. *(Inspecting him)* Practically perfect, your Highness. *(Helps* PRINCE *on with his waistcoat.)*

PRINCE. Tell me, Josef, don't you ever get tired of calling me "Your Highness"? *(Does up his waistcoat with back to* JOSEF.*)*

JOSEF. *(Shocked)* Tired of calling "Your Highness" your Highness? (PRINCE *turns and looks at* JOSEF) Oh, *no,* your Highness.

PRINCE. After all, we're both human beings.

JOSEF. *(Firmly)* No, your Highness, *I* am a human being. Your Highness is a Prince.

PRINCE. *(Laughs)* Have it your own way. (JOSEF *fixes band at back of waistcoat.)* But I sometimes feel that people like me no longer fit into this world. We're anachronisms—forgotten relics of the Middle Ages, through mere oversight left struggling to survive between telephone and radio. Do you know what I need, Josef?

JOSEF. A cocktail.

PRINCE. No. I need extinguishing. I ought to be quickly, but firmly, done away with.

JOSEF. If I might be permitted the liberty——?

PRINCE. Well?

JOSEF. I think your Highness is morbid, if I may use the expression.

PRINCE. Certainly you may use the expression. I *am* morbid. A sign of old age, I suppose.

JOSEF. Your Highness is not old. *(Gets coat off chair and helps* PRINCE *into it.)*

PRINCE. Getting old! Two more grey hairs this morning, Josef.

JOSEF. If I might recommend an excellent preparation——

PRINCE. It wouldn't do any good. There is only one real cure for greying hair. (JOSEF *hands him the handkerchief, which he places in breast pocket of coat.)* It was invented by a Frenchman. He called it the guillotine. (JOSEF *hands* PRINCE *box of flowers.* PRINCE *holds up both flowers and selects white one; puts it in button-hole.* JOSEF *puts box back on* R.C. *table.)* Still to return to a subject we were discussing just now, there are always women——

JOSEF. Yes, your Highness. And ladies, too.

PRINCE. You make a distinction?

JOSEF. Oh, *yes,* your Highness.

PRINCE. Josef, you're a snob.

JOSEF. *(Charmed at the compliment)* Thank you very much, your Highness. *(A BELL rings. JOSEF exits C. to R., using Left door only, and immediately re-enters with CHAUFFEUR, who comes smartly to attention and removes hat with right hand and remains in doorway C.)* Koeppke, your Highness. *(JOSEF comes down to R.C.)*

PRINCE. *(Fills his cigarette case from a box)* Are these the new cigarettes, Josef?

JOSEF. Yes, your Highness.

PRINCE. How do you like them?

JOSEF. A great improvement on the last lot, your Highness.

PRINCE. *(Turns to CHAUFFEUR)* Well, Mercury?

CHAUFFEUR. *(Comes down behind C. chair, clicks his heels and bows. Puzzled)* Your Highness?

PRINCE. Just a flight of imagery. Mercury was the messenger of the gods. You are my messenger, and I am a sort of god. At least, Josef seems to think so.

JOSEF. Just so, your Highness. *(Picks up box of flowers from table R.C. and exits R.)*

PRINCE. Any news?

CHAUFFEUR. Yes, your Highness.

PRINCE. Ah!

CHAUFFEUR. I stopped the car at the opposite curb and waited until the Baron von Reichenheim had left the house—then I went and talked to the janitor.

PRINCE. And then——?

CHAUFFEUR. He let me in, your Highness.

PRINCE. And the flowers?

CHAUFFEUR. I delivered them, your Highness.

PRINCE. To the Baroness herself?

CHAUFFEUR. To the Baroness in person.

PRINCE. It's the same thing.

CHAUFFEUR. Yes, your Highness.

PRINCE. And what did the Baroness—in person—say?

CHAUFFEUR. Nothing, your Highness. She smiled.

PRINCE. Merely smiled?

CHAUFFEUR. Yes, your Highness. (JOSEF *re-enters* R.)

PRINCE. *(Dreamily)* Merely smiled—— A woman's smile—— Now, what the devil was that good thing about woman's smiles that I thought of this morning in my bath? I didn't mention it to you, did I—Josef?

JOSEF. No, your Highness, no.

PRINCE. And now it's gone. Too bad! I always think of my best things in my bath. Tomorrow morning you must come and sit in the bathroom with a notebook. (JOSEF *bows.*) Well, so the lady smiled, did she? And then——

CHAUFFEUR. I smiled, too.

PRINCE. General hilarity, in fact. But she gave you no message to take back to me?

CHAUFFEUR. No, your Highness.

PRINCE. I see. Well, wait for me downstairs. We are going to town. (CHAUFFEUR *clicks heels, bows and exits* C. *to* R., *replacing hat in doorway.*) My fur coat.

JOSEF. *(Bows)* Very good, your Highness. (JOSEF *starts to exit* R.)

PRINCE. *(Crossing to* R. *Meditatively)* Josef— (JOSEF *stops*)—the lady smiled. What do you deduce from that?

JOSEF. She was pleased?

PRINCE. Or amused?

JOSEF. Pleased, your Highness.

PRINCE. You're a great comfort, Josef. You always take the sunny view. Well, one must not expect too much at the first attempt, I suppose.

JOSEF. Rome, your Highness, was not built in a day!

PRINCE. How well you put these things. At any rate, we learn that she is at home and alone. *(He crosses to table L. and picks up telephone directory; sits and hums a tune)* I'll call her. (JOSEF *exits* R. PRINCE *speaks into phone)* Twenty-one-seven-twenty-one, please—— Yes. *(A pause. He speaks dreamily to himself)* The lady smiled—no—not you—— *(Into phone)* Hullo? Is this Twenty-one-seven-twenty-one? May I speak to the Baroness von Rischenheim? What's that? Not at home? (JOSEF *re-enters, carrying fur coat and top hat which he puts on table* L.C.*)* Really, but a few minutes ago she was—— Oh? Indeed? I see—— Thanks—— No, thanks, nothing. I'll call again. *(Puts telephone down. Rises.)*

JOSEF. Your Highness's coat.

PRINCE. Thanks. (JOSEF *helps* PRINCE *into coat.)* Gloves?

JOSEF. In the right-hand pocket, your Highness.

PRINCE. *(Feeling in pocket and producing gloves)* Correct, as always. And now the princely hat, Josef, and we are ready to take his Highness out to dine. (JOSEF *hands him hat.* PRINCE *puts it on)* Thanks. *(Hesitates a moment)* You won't forget to call Fraulein Liserl?

JOSEF. I will attend to it immediately, your Highnes.

PRINCE. Right. *(He goes to door* C. *and pauses.* JOSEF *moves up to* R. *of it and opens other half of door.)* Ha! Got it! A woman's smile is like a bath-tap. Turn it on and you find yourself in hot water. *(Muses a moment)* H'm! Not so damn good, after all. (JOSEF *looks—wondering. Exit* PRINCE, C. *to* R., *followed by* JOSEF. *The sound of front DOOR shutting.)*

(For a moment the stage is empty, then JOSEF *returns; closes door* C. *He takes a cigarette from box, lights it and smokes luxuriantly. Draws the memorandum pad from his pocket, searching for* LISERL'S *address, humming, and reclines on sofa with head toward* C.*)*

JOSEF. Laura—Lina—Lola—Lehmann's Steam Laundry — Liserl — Seventy-eight-Three-Ninety-five. *(Reaches for phone)* Seventy-eight-Three-Ninety-five, please—— Pardon? Seventy-eight—— What? I was ringing Central. Ring off, please. *(Puts phone back in box; takes up phone again)* Seventy-eight-Three-Ninety-five, please. Hullo, is this Central? Well, but that's the—— What number?—What?—Ring off, please. *(Again puts phone back in box, then once more takes up phone)* Hullo? Is this Central? No? What is it? *You* again? For goodness sake—— Can't you—— *(His manner suddenly changes. He has just realized that it is an attractive voice which is speaking—coos)* What a sweet voice you have! *(He listens and smiles)* Me? Oh, *my* voice isn't sweet. No, really? My dear lady, you make me blush. *(With sudden indignation)* A tenor? I'm not a tenor, I'm a light baritone. *(Sweetly once more)* No, of course I'm not offended. Even tenors are God's creatures, aren't they? Ha! Ha! What a delightful laugh you have—— Do go on. Yes, go on laughing. I could listen to you laughing forever. Do you know, I was thinking only this morning that a woman's smile is like a bathtub—tap—— What sort of a man am I? Well, why don't you come around and see?—Oh, do. Pop into your car and come round. I'm a most respectable person. Oh, yes, just a gentleman of leisure. One of the idle rich, you know. Do come and cheer my loneliness. What lovely teeth you have—— Eh? Oh, yes, you can always tell by a woman's voice—what sort of teeth she has. I don't know. It's something in the way she pronounces the word "No". But why say *no?* Oh, don't ring off. Please don't ring off. Those whom Central has joined together let no man put asunder. You can't come? Why not? Your husband out? He must be or you wouldn't be able to stay at the phone so long. You're not sure you want to? But it is your duty. What nobler mission can a woman have than to cheer a lonely man? You *will* come?—Wonderful! Eleven Ringstrasse is the address. Apartment number three on the first floor. Oh, yes, a very exclusive neighborhood. Yes, goodbye. (JOSEF *puts phone back in box and starts* R. *joyfully, unbuttoning his waistcoat. He pauses to turn on the RADIO and then goes out* R. *leaving cigarette off stage, to reappear in a moment, putting on his master's dinner jacket. Lays one decanter of Peach brandy, two cocktail glasses, dishes of preserved ginger, olives, eggs, caviar, salted almonds and grapes—then to radio. He hums the radio melody, then shakes his head and turns it off. He switches on the other station, from which there bursts forth the lecture of some explorer on Terra del Fuego.* JOSEF *stands listening to it* R. *of cabinet. During the radio speech which follows he changes white tie for a black bow, which he produces from pocket of dinner jacket, and ties.*)

RADIO. A maze of Islands—— A wilderness of cleft rocks—out of the track of steamers and seldom visited save by the *yacht* of some wandering millionaire—— That is Terra del Fuego——

JOSEF. Terra del Fuego.

RADIO. The inhabitants of this inhospitable country have a culture of the lowest type——

JOSEF. Fancy.

RADIO. Their compexions are muddy brown, their limbs strikingly short in comparison to the length of their bodies——

JOSEF. Important, if true!

RADIO. They live on raw fungus, snails, roots, sea-slugs and shell-fish——

JOSEF. I can't bear it.

RADIO. Cannibalism, too, is not unknown to them——

JOSEF. What charming people!

RADIO. Though commonly known as Terra del Fuegans the natives are also called Pesceri——

JOSEF. How do you spell that?

RADIO. P-e-s-c-e-r-i——

JOSEF. Thank you very much.

RADIO. I propose to give a short account—if I may——

JOSEF. You may *not*. (JOSEF *switches back to other station which plays "Viennese Potpouri" Part I. After a count of six, front DOORBELL rings.* JOSEF *closes door of loud speaker and exits* C., *opening both doors wide. The stage is empty for a moment, then* JOSEF *appears and stands in passage to* L. *of double doors.* MARIE *appears in doorway, very elegantly dressed, with sable wrap.* JOSEF *closes doors after her entrance and after looking admiringly at her, while she walks slowly down* C., *he switches off radio, leaving top of cabinet open. He approaches on her right and takes* MARIE'S *hand. She withdraws it quickly.*)

MARIE. *(Down* L.C.*)* Please——

JOSEF. *(*C.*)* I'm sorry——

MARIE. I suppose you think I'm——

JOSEF. Oh, no.

MARIE. What?

JOSEF. Nothing—nothing. How can I think when I see you standing there? The brain refuses to function.

MARIE. *(Looking about her)* So I really am here.

JOSEF. *(Tenderly)* Really here.

MARIE. *(Quickly—crosses to him* C.*)* But I've only come to say I can't come.

JOSEF. Of course.

MARIE. You see—my husband——

JOSEF. Oh! Please! Please! Isn't there enough sorrow in the world without thinking of your husband?

MARIE. *(Backs)* Well, thank you so much for a lovely evening. *(Gives him her hand.)*

JOSEF. You're not going? *(Taking it.)*

MARIE. Of course I'm going. *(Sits in armchair* C.*)* Goodbye. Never, never before have I set foot in a strange gentleman's apartment. If anyone had told me an hour ago that I would have behaved like this, I should have laughed.

JOSEF. Won't you now?

MARIE. What?

JOSEF. Laugh. You have such a delightful laugh. *(After a pause of hesitation,* MARIE *laughs.* JOSEF *laughs, too)* There, that's better. *(He attempts to take her hand. She draws it away.)*

MARIE. But you're forgetting I don't know where I am.

JOSEF. Don't you know really?

MARIE. Of course not.

JOSEF. Do you mean to say you don't really know whose apartment this is?

MARIE. How should I? Whose is it?

JOSEF. It belongs to Prince Rudolf Haseldorf.

MARIE. Oh, you're a prince. Fancy that!

JOSEF. *(Nonchalantly)* Yes. You think Princes important?

MARIE. Oh, *but*—of course I do.

JOSEF. I don't. I was saying as much to my man not long ago. "Tell me, Josef," I said to him: "Don't you ever get tired of saying 'Your Highness'? After all, we're both human beings."

MARIE. But how terribly broadminded of you!

JOSEF. You think so? Oh, I don't know. *(Laughs deprecatingly)* I sometimes feel that people like me no longer fit into this world.

MARIE. Oh, *no*.

JOSEF. We are—er—anachronisms—forgotten relics of the Middle Ages, through mere oversight left struggling to survive between telephone and radio.

MARIE. What sort is yours?

JOSEF. Mine?

MARIE. Yes, the radio.

JOSEF. Oh, that thing. That's a Sonora.

MARIE. Oh, really. So is ours. *(Laughs.)*

JOSEF. Really? *(Tenderly—leans over her)* How close that seems to bring us together. *(Tries to take her hand.)*

MARIE. *(Drawing back)* Oh! I'm afraid you're a ladies' man, Prince.

JOSEF. *No*, no.

MARIE. Oh, but you are. I could tell it at once.

JOSEF. Could you? How?

MARIE. Your eyes have that strange, wild gleam.

JOSEF. Oh, no, no! Have they really?

MARIE. The gleam of the typical Lothario.

JOSEF. Let me remove your wrap.

MARIE. Oh, no, no, no. *(Rises and crosses to table* R.C.*)* Didn't I say I was just going?

JOSEF. Yes, yes, of course you did. But it's so cold out of doors. If you left suddenly, you might catch a chill.

MARIE. Well! Perhaps you're right. (JOSEF *removes* MARIE'S *wrap, as she slips it off. She turns. Sits* L. *of* R.C. *table and LIGHT comes up on her. Spot from 1st border.)*

JOSEF. *(Looking at* MARIE*)* Wonderful! Just as my fancy pictured you. I never realized before how distinctly I can see a woman over the phone. *(Sits* *on arm of* C. *chair)* And now may I be permitted to learn your name?

MARIE. Oh—— Well, if you must know, it's Marie. *(She takes handkerchief out of handbag.)*

JOSEF. *(Tenderly)* Marie? Yes, charming, go on.

MARIE. That's all. That's all there is. There isn't any more. *(They laugh) I* say, may I have a little liqueur?

JOSEF. Of course, I beg your pardon. *(Crosses to* R. *of table; puts cloak on back of chair—pours* MARIE *out a glass.)*

MARIE. What is it?

JOSEF. *(Hands her glass)* Peach brandy.

MARIE. Oh! How lovely! *(While* JOSEF *is pouring out his)* How *expertly* you pour—you didn't spill a drop——

JOSEF. What? Oh, yes! One picks up these things from watching one's man.

MARIE. I see. *(They drink.)*

JOSEF. *(Sits* R. *of table facing her)* Marie—what a charming name——

MARIE. *(Sips)* It's nice.

JOSEF. It is, indeed.

MARIE. I mean the liqueur——

JOSEF. Oh! I beg your pardon.

MARIE. And what a delightful place you have here.

JOSEF. Not so bad.

MARIE. Perfectly charming.

JOSEF. I gave the decorators carte blanche. "Money is no object," I said. *(He sips the drink.)*

MARIE. You're not married, of course?

JOSEF. How on earth did you guess that?

MARIE. Because you live on the first floor— *(Again sips drink)*—bachelors always live on the first floor.

JOSEF. You have no objection to bachelors, I hope?

MARIE. No. Of course, they're selfish.
JOSEF. Selfish?
MARIE. Yes, you see, what I always say is, a bachelor is just a man who is cheating some nice woman out of a divorce. (BOTH *laugh*) So you are all alone here?
JOSEF. Eh? Oh, yes, yes—all alone. Except for my servant. But you needn't worry about him, I have sent him out and he always stops out late.
MARIE. Now, what do you mean by that? You surely don't suppose I am going to stay *here* more than five minutes?
JOSEF. Of course not. Have some more brandy? *(Refills her glass which she holds up.)*
MARIE. Well, ten minutes at the outside.
JOSEF. Ten minutes of Paradise. Tell me, does your husband call you Marie?
MARIE. Of course.
JOSEF. Does he really? I thought he might call you Mary, or Marion or Maria or Mitzie. *(Sips again.)*
MARIE. *(Laughs)* Oh, Mitzie. Oh, I'm quite giggly! *(Rises; glances about room; sees photograph —up* L.C.*)* Oh, oh, oh! Now, now. A lady! Who is she?
JOSEF. *(Rises)* Er—distant aunt of mine.
MARIE. *(Crosses up and picks it up)* Is she really? Why, it's the Queen of Rumania.
JOSEF. *(Crosses up* C. *Takes it from her)* What! Why, so it is! I do seem to remember hearing something about her marrying the King of Rumania. *(Dusts the photograph.)*
MARIE. What *are* you doing?
JOSEF. *(Embarrassed)* Excuse me. Just an old family custom.
MARIE. I see. *(Crosses back to her chair and sits)* You dust as well as you pour brandy.
JOSEF. *(Places photo on radio cabinet up* R.C.*)*

Yes, all my family have been great dusters. *(He closes top of radio. Quickly)* Have something more to drink?

MARIE. Oh, I wouldn't dare!

JOSEF. Something to eat? Caviar on toast? Grapes? Cake? An egg? Anything you please. Do try some caviar.

MARIE. No, I don't like caviar. *(Takes plate from top of table.)*

JOSEF. No?

MARIE. I can't bear it.

JOSEF. There, you see, and I love it. Strange how tastes differ, isn't it?

MARIE. Amazing!

JOSEF. I remember the last time I was in Terra del Fuego——

MARIE. Oh! Have you been to Terra del Fuego?

JOSEF. Oh, yes. Yachting, you know. *(Takes an egg and starts to remove shell.)*

MARIE. Yes, I *suppose* you *must* be a great traveler.

JOSEF. Oh, one gets about. I was saying that the natives of Terra del Fuego prefer the most unappetizing articles of food——

MARIE. *(Not listening)* So your name is Rudolf?

JOSEF. Yes, Rudolf.

MARIE. Rudolf—— I like it.

JOSEF. You do? Thanks, but after all, what's in a name?

MARIE. A mere bagatelle. *(Takes a handful of olives.)*

JOSEF. The Terra del Fuegans are also called Pesceri.

MARIE. Really? How do you spell it?

JOSEF. P-e-s-c-e-r-i.

MARIE. Thank you very much.

JOSEF. They have a culture of the lowest type and muddy brown complexions——

MARIE. *(Examining food)* What's this?

JOSEF. Eh? Oh—that's candied ginger.

MARIE. *(Nibbles ginger)* Ooh, it's hot. *(Sips drink.)*

JOSEF. Yes. A Terra del Fuegan wouldn't like it at all.

MARIE. No. I don't like it very much myself.

JOSEF. What they prefer are roots, shellfish, snails, sea-slugs and funguses.

MARIE. I see. Just a simple cold buffet. *(Helps herself to another glass of brandy, filling it too full—has to stoop to sip it.* BOTH *laugh.)*

JOSEF. Cannibalism, too, is not unknown to them.

MARIE. To whom?

JOSEF. The Terra del Fuegans..

MARIE. *Oh,* really. *Well,* go on, tell me what else do you know about the Terra del Fuegans.

JOSEF. What else? Well—er—— No, no, don't let's talk about Terra del Fuegans. Let us talk about ourselves. Are you still sorry you came?

MARIE. *(Coyly)* Do you want to hear the truth? *(Places hand on table.)*

JOSEF. I have no objection to the truth—in moderation.

MARIE. Well, then, I'm *not* sorry.

JOSEF. *(Rises, taking her hand)* Marie!

MARIE. Rudolf! (JOSEF *is about to kiss her hand when the DOORBELL rings.* JOSEF *sits again.)* Someone at the door?

JOSEF. *(Frightfully embarrassed)* Someone at the door!

MARIE. I wonder who it is?

JOSEF. I der—der—don't know.

(BELL rings again.)

MARIE. Well, hadn't you better find out?

JOSEF. Per—per—possibly.

MARIE. *(Suddenly alarmed)* Oh! *(Jumps up; crosses to* C. *and turns to him.* JOSEF, *startled, jumps up violently.)* Suppose it's someone looking for me?

JOSEF. Good Lord!

MARIE. I may have been followed. *(Comes R. for her cloak and goes toward R. door.* JOSEF *with hands to head crosses below her to C.)*

JOSEF. *(Taking her hand and pulling her to door L.)* No, no. Don't go in there. Go in here!

MARIE. *(Nervous)* What is it?

JOSEF. Only the smoking room.

MARIE. *(Crossing to door L.)* Don't be long. I'm frightened to death. *(Turns at door)* I've never done this sort of thing before in my life. (MARIE *exits L., taking cloak with her.)*

JOSEF. Don't worry, I won't keep you a moment. *(BELL rings again.* JOSEF *hesitates R. hastily starting to remove coat and exits R. BELL rings again.* JOSEF *enters R., putting on livery and crosses up to C. off R., opening L. half of door only.)*

LISERL. *(Enters C., speaking as she enters and crossing C.)* His Highness not here? I don't believe a word of it.

JOSEF. *(Stands behind* LISERL *on her L.)* Do you think I would deceive you, madame?

LISERL. No. But I think you might try.

JOSEF. His Highness is really out.

LISERL. But he was expecting me.

JOSEF. His Highness instructed me to say that he asks a thousand pardons, but he was unfortunately compelled, much against his will——

LISERL. *(Satirically)* Stop me, if you've heard this before!

JOSEF. No, really, madame. It's the literal truth.

LISERL. Truth? You couldn't tell the truth even in your diary.

JOSEF. His Excellency, Count Holsten, insisted on His Highness meeting an old friend from England.

LISERL. Oh! What's her name?

JOSEF. A gentleman, madame, not a lady.

LISERL. Well, it's nice of you to bother to make up a good story for me. Thank you.

JOSEF. Don't mention it, madame.

LISERL. So what you want me to believe is that his Highness has gone out and didn't even consider it worth while to tell me?

JOSEF. You wrong his Highness, madame. He instructed me to telephone you, but—*(Looks at phone)*—er—well, something went wrong with the telephone.

LISERL. Indeed? Well, I'll wait.

JOSEF. *(Aghast)* Wait, here?

LISERL. Right here.

JOSEF. But you can't!

LISERL. Watch me! *(Sits L. of R.C. table and drops her cloak over back of chair.)*

JOSEF. But his Highness may be late.

LISERL. Well, I'll be later. *(Noticing table is laid—places her bag on table.)*

JOSEF. *(Aside)* I'll be damned!

LISERL. Oh! Someone's been eating. Eggs!

JOSEF. Er—yes. Just before he was going out, his Highness hastily snatched an egg——

LISERL. Before going out to dinner?

JOSEF. He always eats an egg before going out to dinner. Doctor's orders.

LISERL. Well, what the doctor orders is good enough for me. I'm starving. *(Takes a piece of ginger; rises; crosses to settee L. and starts to eat.* JOSEF *glances despairingly at door L.)* Josef!

JOSEF. Madame?

LISERL. Don't call me "Madame". Call me Liserl.

JOSEF. Call you Liserl?

LISERL. Yes. Josef, his Highness is untrue to me.

JOSEF. Impossible.

LISERL. He is. I can tell by the eggs.

JOSEF. Not so loud, please.
LISERL. *(Sits on settee)* Do you think I'm a fool?
JOSEF. Yes. I mean, no.
LISERL. I will have my revenge.
JOSEF. Perhaps there is some message I can give his Highness?
LISERL. Yes. Tell him he can go to the devil.
JOSEF. I beg your pardon?
LISERL. He can go to the devil, and you can come here and kiss me.
JOSEF. Madame!
LISERL. Come here!
JOSEF. But, madame——
LISERL. Sit down. (JOSEF *looks at* L. *door, frightened—crosses and sits down on settee.*) There! When his Highness returns he shall find us together—*(Puts arm around him)*—like this.
JOSEF. But, Madame, think of the difference in our social positions.
LISERL. I'm not a snob.
JOSEF. No, but I am.
LISERL. Oh! Don't you like me?
JOSEF. Oh, yes, madame, in a spirit of proper respect.
LISERL. I like you.
JOSEF. Thank you, madame. But——
LISERL. But what?
JOSEF. Please control yourself. Please have a little consideration for me. *(Rises and stands at the end of the settee.)*
LISERL. Are you a Josef by nature as well as by name?
JOSEF. It is a question of conscience, madame.
LISERL. Conscience!
JOSEF. I enjoy his Highness's confidence and trust and—er——
LISERL. And what?

28 CANDLE-LIGHT ACT I

JOSEF. I really couldn't take the liberty of—er—taking a liberty——
LISERL. Oh, you mean you never poach.
JOSEF. Only eggs, madame.
LISERL. *(Rises; crosses to* C.*)* Oh, all right, all right. Well, I'm off then. Tell his Highness I shall not call again. *(Puts on cloak.)*
JOSEF. I regret deeply if I have proved a disappointment. *(Crosses to behind armchair* C.*)*
LISERL. *(Coldly)* Disappointment? Surely you're not foolish enough to imagine that I was serious? *(Picks up bag from* R.C. *table.)*
JOSEF. I—er—did somehow get the impression——
LISERL. The very idea! I would have you know, my man,—*(Crossing to* C. *door)*—that I am a good woman, a very good woman! *(In doorway)* By the way, the last time I was here I left my pajamas—you can send them on to me. *(Exit* LISERL, *followed by* JOSEF C. *to* R.*)*
JOSEF. *(As he goes)* His Highness will be inconsolable—— *(The front door SLAMS.* JOSEF *hurries back; closes the doors and exits* R.*; changes his coat; enters and crosses to* L. *door and opens it)* I say, I'm terribly sorry. Please forgive me.
MARIE. *(Enters; crosses to* C.*)* Well! Nice goings on, I must say!
JOSEF. I'm awfully sorry. I beg your pardon.
MARIE. What sort of a place is this?
JOSEF. *(Following her)* I beg a thousand pardons——
MARIE. *(Turns and* JOSEF *takes cloak off her arm.)* There seem to be women in every nook and cranny.
JOSEF. I assure you that the unfortunate occurrence will not occur again. (MARIE *crosses and puts bag on* R.C. *table)* You see, as a matter of fact, the lady was the very lady I was trying to speak to on

the telephone, to cancel our appointment, when Fate connected me with you.

MARIE. *(Crosses back to* C.*)* Oh, you were going to cancel the appointment?

JOSEF. Yes. Kindly but firmly.

MARIE. I suppose you were tired of her?

JOSEF. Well, frankly her society *had* begun to occasion me a slight ennui.

MARIE. Really? Why?

JOSEF. Please! One must be discreet.

MARIE. I wonder how long you remain faithful to one woman?

JOSEF. The period varies. Sometimes it is very short, but sometimes——

MARIE. Even shorter?

JOSEF. I could be true forever—to the right woman.

MARIE. *(Sighs)* Oh! You men! How lucky you men are! You sit cosily at home, like *spiders* in your webs, and the poor little flies come buzzing in one after another. *(Crosses to* R.C. *table and picks up her glass)* Who knows how many have already been here, in this very room——

JOSEF. *(Waving his hand vaguely)* Oh——

MARIE. Only great ladies, of course. A man like you wouldn't bother about anything lower than a Baroness. *(Drinks.)*

JOSEF. One *is* rather exclusive.

MARIE. An affair with a plain, ordinary, simple girl wouldn't *interest* Prince Rudolf.

JOSEF. It would bore Prince Rudolf most frightfully.

MARIE. I think you're terrible.

JOSEF. Don't say that. *(Approaches and takes hold of her)* You know you don't really mean it.

MARIE. *(Disengaging herself)* Perhaps I don't.

JOSEF. That's better. I know you didn't. Come

now, won't you sit down and tell me all about yourself? *(She sits L. of table and puts down glass. JOSEF crosses behind and places cloak on chair R. of table and returns to C.)* Do you realize that all I know at present is your first name?

MARIE. Surely isn't that enough—to go on with?

JOSEF. Of course, I quite understand. You want to conceal your identity. (MARIE *looks up nervously.*) Yours is an aristocratic—possibly even a world-famous—name——

MARIE. To you it is simply "Marie."

JOSEF. *(Fondly)* Marie!

MARIE. You know how it is. Here I do not wish to be the great lady—— Just try and look upon me as that plain, ordinary simple girl. (JOSEF *laughs.*) That amuses you? *(Makes a grimace; takes out compact and powders her face.)*

JOSEF. I should say it does. You—a girl like that? Why, I can tell that you move in the very highest circles.

MARIE. *(Eagerly)* You can?

JOSEF. At a glance. *(Commences to walk to L. and sits on R. arm of C. chair.)*

MARIE. How?

JOSEF. By your voice.

MARIE. Oh, I see. Just by the sound of my voice! Fancy that. You know, I think you are awfully nice.

JOSEF. Oh! Do you really?

MARIE. Oh, yes.

JOSEF. Really!

MARIE. *(Powders her nose)* Oh, you're so much nicer than the men one usually meets at social functions.

JOSEF. Really? How you must shine at those social functions! Do you have many of them?

MARIE. *Oh,* yes, we entertain extensively. Hundreds of guests—luncheons, dinners, suppers and all that. But it's a great bore. Men have such a way of being attentive to one.

JOSEF. Impetuous?

MARIE. Importunate!

JOSEF. Impossible!

MARIE. And it's so difficult *to snub* them. Of course, one wants to be virtuous.

JOSEF. Why? I mean——

MARIE. *Well,* it's so difficult. When one is young——

JOSEF. And beautiful.

MARIE. Yes, one is rather, isn't one? You know, domesticity becomes so tedious. Always the same husband.

JOSEF. Yes, I know.

MARIE. If you knew the eternal quarrels *about* my extravagances.

JOSEF It's too bad.

MARIE. And I'm not extravagant.

JOSEF. No. No.

MARIE. Time after time rather than exceed my allowance—I've had things charged. I often say that the servants have the best time.

JOSEF. *(Starting)* The servants—— *(Rises and moves L.)*

MARIE. They are much freer. Aren't they?

JOSEF. Oh, you mean because they're not married?

MARIE. Ah! Yes, of course, *there's that,* too.

JOSEF. *(Crosses back to C.)* Yes. Tell me, if your husband knew that you were here—what would he do?

MARIE. *(Half rising)* Oh! I tremble to think of it. Do you know—he wouldn't leave this room except over your dead body. *(Starts to eat nuts, etc.)*

JOSEF. *(Uncomfortably) Wouldn't* he? Wouldn't

he, indeed? That's very interesting—er—tell me is he a big man?

MARIE. Yes. He's huge. *(Picks up glass.)*

JOSEF. And jealous?

MARIE. As jealous as Othello. *(She drinks.)*

JOSEF. As Othello! Othello?

MARIE. Surely you've heard of Othello?

JOSEF. Of course, of course.

MARIE. In the play, you know.

JOSEF. Ah, yes, in the play.

MARIE. Haven't you seen the play Othello?

JOSEF. Have you?

MARIE. I can't say I have. *(They laugh.)*

JOSEF. *(Relieved)* Ah! *(Crosses to L. below settee.)*

MARIE. But you've turned *quite* white. Honestly, I *believe* you are frightened.

JOSEF. I—frightened? I would fight the whole world for you.

MARIE. Splendid!

JOSEF. Er—if necessary. *(They laugh)* Shall we take a little stroll through the apartment?

MARIE. *(Rises; leaves her bag on table)* I'd love it. *(They cross up back C.)*

JOSEF. The smoking room you have already seen. This we call the den.

MARIE. Why?

JOSEF. I don't know why. Furnished in the modern style. *(Leads MARIE across hall and opens double doors)* This is the library. The library consists entirely of books.

MARIE. *(On L. of JOSEF)* I don't believe you.

JOSEF. Do you like books?

MARIE. I adore books.

JOSEF. I have yards and yards of books.

MARIE. Have you?

JOSEF. Quite a yard and a half of Shakespeare alone——

MARIE. Shakespeare? My goodness, is *that* man still writing? *(They exit into library R.C., she on L., he on R., and leave open doors behind them. For a moment the stage remains empty.)*

(The PRINCE *enters C. from R., removing gloves, and crosses to behind C. chair. He turns and exhibits surprise at finding the room illuminated. He removes hat and puts it on R.C. table, puts gloves in hat, notices table still set and seeing bag, picks it up.)*

MARIE. *(Is heard off)* Prince, you mustn't! Really you mustn't!

(PRINCE *starts, drops bag and looks up. More LAUGHTER is heard, and* PRINCE, *moving up C., stops. He turns and starts to exit R., when he remembers his hat, picks it up and exits R.* MARIE *and* JOSEF *come out of library, to C.)*

MARIE. You must behave yourself. You promised *me* you'd behave.

JOSEF. I *am* behaving.

MARIE. I know you are here. But in there——

JOSEF. It was only your neck. And only for an instant.

MARIE. *(Sits on arm of chair C.)* I was looking at such an interesting book. The illustrations! My word!—Who was *it* by?

JOSEF. I've no idea.

MARIE. But surely you *must* know your own books?

JOSEF. *(Close to her, bending over)* Oh, of course, of course, certainly. Know them all by heart. But I didn't notice which book it was. I stood behind you and saw only you.

MARIE. Yes and you kissed only me. *(Rises and moves toward L. table.)*

JOSEF. How I would like to go on kissing only you forever. Shall I tell you something?

MARIE. You'd better not.   *(WARN Curtain.)*

JOSEF. I love you. I'll love you for ever and ever.

MARIE. How monotonous! *(Crosses; sits in c. chair)* Besides, think of my husband.

JOSEF. Please. Is this the time to think of husbands?

MARIE. I should have thought it was just the time.

JOSEF. I hate your husband. *(She laughs.)* I've never met him, but I hate him. I know exactly the sort of man he is. Cold, brutal, neglectful. I know the type—there you sit at hime waiting for him. He promised to love and honor you, and you see him for about an hour a day.

MARIE. Oh, *well,* an hour soon passes.

JOSEF. *(Kneels by her; takes her hand)* Let me teach you what it means really to be loved.

MARIE. You men are all alike. You all say the same old thing.

JOSEF. I give you my word of honor——

MARIE. That's about all any of you ever do give a girl.

JOSEF. I swear——

MARIE. You all swear. (JOSEF *kisses her hand. He tries to draw* MARIE *to him and kiss her.)*

(Enter the PRINCE, R. *He is wearing* JOSEF's *livery. He holds a tray with coffee cups on it.)*

PRINCE. Shall I serve the coffee here, your Highness?

(JOSEF *turns and slowly rises.* MARIE *indicates* L.

table to PRINCE. *The* PRINCE *crosses to behind table* L. *with a very serious and discreet air. Turns and looks at the* OTHERS. JOSEF *watches him, aghast.* MARIE *eyes the* PRINCE.)

CURTAIN

ACT TWO

SCENE: *The same.*

TIME: *A few minutes later.*
Both C. *doors are open through this Act. Door curtains have been slightly drawn to cover jambs of doors.*

JOSEF has gone into the library to find a book. The PRINCE is clearing the table, and during the scene removes two glasses, one decanter, two plates.

The chair from L. *of table is now at the head of it, and* MARIE'S *cloak is on chair* R. *of table as at end of Act I.*

AT RISE: MARIE, *sitting in armchair* C., *reading paper, looks at* PRINCE *with a meditative smile. she rises and crosses to table* L. *and takes a cigarette from humidor and looks about for a light. The* PRINCE *comes quickly to her.*

PRINCE. *(Getting lighter out of his pocket as he crosses)* Permit me, Madame. *(Lights* MARIE'S *cigarette.)*

MARIE. Thank you. (PRINCE *crosses back to* R.C. *table, clearing same.)* By the way, what's your name?

PRINCE. Josef, madame.

MARIE. Josef, have you been in the Prince's service long?

PRINCE. Quite a considerable time, madame.

MARIE. I suppose you take care of him very well?

36

ACT II   CANDLE-LIGHT   37

PRINCE. I endeavor to do so, madame. In fact, I may say the sole object of my life is to minister to his Higheness's slightest whim.
MARIE. Yes, I shouldn't think there are many servants like you, Josef.
PRINCE. Very few, I should imagine.
MARIE. I see he'd be in a bad way if you left him.
PRINCE. He would indeed.
MARIE. *(Crosses to* C. *chair)* Tell me about him, Josef.
PRINCE. There is not much to tell, madame. I should describe his Highness as a man who means well, but does not always do what he means—who has ideals but generally fails——
MARIE. *(Impatiently)* No, no. I don't mean that, Josef. I mean, tell me about his private life.
PRINCE. Really, madame——
MARIE. Oh, now, don't be so coy. *(Crosses for her bag which is now on* L. *table)* Here! *(Takes a coin from bag)* Perhaps this will help to loosen your tongue. *(Returns to* C. *armchair.)*
PRINCE. *(Startled)* Oh, I say, no! Really, hang it all.
MARIE. What?
PRINCE. I mean, his Highness does not like me to accept tips.
MARIE. What—never?
PRINCE. Never from ladies, madame.
MARIE. Don't be ridiculous. *(Throws bag on settee)* Here—take it. *(Offers coin.)*
PRINCE. No—— Please—— Really——
MARIE. Oh, now, come on. Perhaps it will be easier for you this way. Here—— *(Thrusts coin into the* PRINCE'S *hand)* There, isn't that better? *(*PRINCE *shrugs and pockets it.* MARIE *sits* C.*)* Now, then, tell me all. In the first place, have you a mistress?
PRINCE. I *beg your* pardon.

MARIE. I mean—is the Prince married?

PRINCE. Oh, I see. No, madame. He is a bachelor.

MARIE. So he told me, but I thought I'd make sure. And has he any particular—playmate?

PRINCE. No, madame. He just flits from flower to flower.

MARIE. Yes, I should think he's the sort of a man who has a regular regiment of women on his books.

PRINCE. They do pile up.

MARIE. I should say they do. Do you know what happened just now, Josef?

PRINCE. No, madame.

MARIE. I came to pay him a visit—in a nice way, of course——

PRINCE. Of course.

MARIE. And I hadn't been here five minutes before all the skeletons in his cupboard started parading in front of me.

PRINCE. Madame?

MARIE. I mean—another woman arrived.

PRINCE. She did?

MARIE. She certainly did. Have you any idea who she was, Josef?

PRINCE. I regret I have no information on the point, madame.

MARIE. Well, she must have been a friend of his, because he threw her out.

PRINCE. He did?

MARIE. He certainly did. Lipstick, toothbrush, pajamas and everything! Whoosh! *(She rises, puts paper on settee and stands* R. *of* L. *table)* Josef, I don't think this place is respectable.

PRINCE. (C. *Meditatively)* Now, I wonder who that could have been.

(Enter JOSEF *from the library; crosses down* R. *of* R.C. *table. He looks worried and nervous.)*

MARIE. *(Rises)* Hello, Prince. Did you find the book?

JOSEF. Not yet.

MARIE. But we had it a minute ago. Don't you remember? I was reading it in the library when you kissed me on the back of the neck.

JOSEF. *(Agitated)* Sssh! *(Moves down in front of table.* JOSEF *catches* PRINCE'S *eye and wriggles uncomfortably.* PRINCE *turns aside to hide a smile.)* Well! You must have put it somewhere.

PRINCE. If I may be permitted to inquire, which is the volume under discussion? What did the book look like?

MARIE. It's very large and full of illustrations.

PRINCE. In color.

MARIE. No. Off-color.

PRINCE. I don't know. Were they copper-plate?

MARIE. *(To* JOSEF*) Were* they copper-plate?

JOSEF. *(Confused)* Copper—or nickel—I don't remember.

MARIE. Well, the artist ought to be ashamed of himself, and I'd like another look at them. *(Sits* C.*)*

PRINCE. If your Highness will permit me, I will institute a search. *(Crosses up* C*)*.

MARIE. That's right, Josef, you feel along the shelves, until something burns your fingers and that'll be it. *(Exit* PRINCE *into library and to* R., *leaving door of library open.)* What a charming man that is!

JOSEF. *(Sits at head of table—mopping his forehead)* Phew!

MARIE. Whatever's the matter? You seem nervous.

JOSEF. *(Jumps up)* I'm not nervous. *(Crosses down* R. *and below table to* C.*)* But why on earth must you be bothering about that confounded book? Did you really come here just to inspect the library?

MARIE. You needn't be so cross.

JOSEF. I'm not cross. *(Walking up and down* C.*)*
MARIE. Yes, you are cross. Biting my head off!
JOSEF. *(Hysterically)* I didn't bite your head off.
MARIE. *(Losing some of her artificial polish as she starts to quarrel)* But you did bite my head off. And a little while ago everything was so nice and cozy.
JOSEF. Yes, and now *he* has to come back.
MARIE. Well, what difference does that make?
JOSEF. It's too bad. Really, it's too bad. *(Walks down* R. *and up to back* C. *and down again)* I give the fellow—I give the fellow the evening off—and he comes back and embarrasses me like this.
MARIE. Good gracious! Why should he embarrass you? Treat him as thin air.
JOSEF. Oh! I wish I could.
MARIE. He's not disturbing us.
JOSEF. Yes, he is. It—er—breaks the spell, his being here. It spoils the romance, the poetry.
MARIE. Then why don't you send him to bed?
JOSEF. *(Is now* C.*)* At eight o'clock? *(Bending over her)* Do you think you could get that fellow into bed at eight o'clock?
MARIE. *(Demurely)* I don't know. I might try.
JOSEF. He never goes to bed at all. He only starts getting lively at night. The later *it* gets, the livelier he gets.
MARIE. Well, if his presence annoys you, why on earth don't you fire him?
JOSEF. Ssh! *Please!*

(Re-enter PRINCE, *leaving library door open and carrying book under his left arm to* C. JOSEF *is below* R.C. *table.)*

PRINCE. *Primitive Passion.*
MARIE. I beg your pardon.

PRINCE. *(Hands book to her)* Is that the book you want?
MARIE. *(Taking it)* Well, it *sounds* just like the book I want—thank you—Josef.
PRINCE. Madame is welcome.
MARIE. *(Opens and looks at book)* No, this isn't the same book, but it's the same temperature. *(To* JOSEF*)* I say, on second thought—*don't* you fire him. He's very intelligent.
PRINCE. *(Suavely, to* JOSEF*)* Was your Highness thinking of dismissing me?
JOSEF. What—no, no—— Oh, no. (PRINCE *crosses up to* L. *of* C. *doors.)*
MARIE. *(Rises, puts cigarette in ashtray on* L. *table, and crosses to* JOSEF*)* Well, I'll leave you. *(Then aside, to* JOSEF*)* Send him to bed while I've gone.
JOSEF. Eh?
MARIE. *(Whispers)* Him—bed. *(Indicates sleep in dumb show and crosses up. Walks toward back* C.*)* I'm going back into the library. You know, this is the sort of book one should only read in solitary confinement. (MARIE *exits into library, closing library door.)*
JOSEF. *(Below table* R.C., *is trying to escape by* R. *door and* PRINCE *beckons him back)* Your Highness, how can I explain?
PRINCE. *(Croses down* C.*)* No need. The situation explains itself.
JOSEF. *(Crosses to* R.C.*)* Let me send her away?
PRINCE. Well, really, my dear Josef, if that's the sort of woman you are in the habit of lightly sending away, you must have become very blasé of late.
JOSEF. Your Highness, I don't know what to say— I don't know how such a thing could have happened.
PRINCE. *(Moves toward* C. *chair)* I am the one to blame. I shouldn't have come home so early.

JOSEF. Exactly. *(Corrects himself quickly)* I mean——

PRINCE. Still, I do think you might have told me that you were expecting a visitor.

JOSEF. But I wasn't.

PRINCE. You mean you didn't know she was coming?

JOSEF I hadn't the slightest idea. I was never so surprised in my life.

PRINCE. Indeed? Well, I have no objection to your being surprised, but was it necessary to be surprised in *my* coat?

JOSEF. Your Highness may rest assured that only the most vital necessity compelled me to borrow your Highness's coat. You see, your Highness, this lady is a real lady. She moves in the highest circles. Entertains! Hundreds of guests! I couldn't let her know I was just your valet.

PRINCE. Well, I suppose it *would* have cast a damper on the proceedings.

JOSEF. Exactly, your Highness. *(PRINCE feels for cigarette case. JOSEF offers one from the PRINCE's own case, which he produces from the pocket of the coat he is wearing. PRINCE shows surprise.)* Allow me, your Highness.

PRINCE. *(Takes cigarette)* But how on earth did you happen to come across this woman?

JOSEF. *(Crosses to table L., strikes match and lights PRINCE's cigarette)* Over the telephone, your Highness. (PRINCE *looks at him.*) Quite unexpectedly I found myself talking to her. And you know how you talk nonsense on the telephone.

PRINCE. *(Again looks at him)* Eh?

JOSEF. I mean—er—it is just possible that I may have said something which sounded like an invitation—(PRINCE *sits* C. JOSEF *stands* L. *of him)*—purely in a spirit of wholesome fun, and I'd hardly put down the receiver when there she was ringing the front doorbell.

PRINCE. With women, my dear Josef, one must be prepared for anything.

JOSEF. Is that so, your Highness?

PRINCE. Certainly. Don't you know anything about women?

JOSEF. Your Highness, I don't even suspect anything.

PRINCE. Odd, that she should have come so quickly. Her home must be near here.

JOSEF. Let me send her away?

PRINCE. Certainly not. I am surprised at you, Josef. For the first time in your life you find yourself in the middle of a real romance and you want to end it.

JOSEF. Yes. But now that your Highness has returned——

PRINCE. My Highness has not returned. My Highness has been here all the time, kissing the lady on the back of the neck, I gather. It is Josef who has returned.

JOSEF. But surely your Highness does not intend to keep up the deception—to let the lady go on thinking I am you and you are me?

PRINCE. Why not? Your clothes fit me splendidly.

JOSEF. Your Highness always did have a perfect figure.

PRINCE. *(Bows)* You have always been a good servant to me—(JOSEF *bows*)—so now I will serve you. It's only fair you should have your turn.

JOSEF. Yes, but your Highness——

PRINCE. Don't worry, I shall enjoy it. We'll play this game out together. For the rest of the evening *you* shall be the Prince and *I* the valet.

JOSEF. If your Highness really will consent just for a few hours—it would be a great kindness.

PRINCE. Rely on me. I take it the lady attracts you, Josef?

JOSEF. Oh! Your Highness, she makes me feel like one of the great lovers of history.

PRINCE. You never soared to such exalted heights before?

JOSEF. Never, your Highness. Just cooks and ladies' maids, with perhaps a governess at Christmas.

PRINCE. I understand, Josef.

JOSEF. An adventure with a real lady—— Your Highness, it means so much to me. Such looks, such style——

PRINCE. And such generosity.

JOSEF. Eh?

PRINCE. Just now she tipped me.

JOSEF. *(Shocked)* Tipped *you*, your Highness!

PRINCE. *(Taking out coin)* Here you are. I hand it on.

JOSEF. Oh, your Highness—— No—I couldn't take it!

PRINCE. Well, you don't expect *me* to keep it?

JOSEF. But from her, your Highness—a tip from her—from the woman—the lady—I love.

PRINCE. All right, I'll toss you for it.

JOSEF. No, no.

PRINCE. Then keep it as a souvenir. *(Tosses it to him.)*

JOSEF. *(Catching it)* A souvenir—— Ah, well, of course—— *(Looks at it)* Looking at it like that——

PRINCE. —you might make it harmonize with your great passion.

JOSEF. I could try. *(Pockets coin)* But, your Highness—don't you really think we had better send her away?

PRINCE. Over my dead body. (JOSEF *winces.*) What's the matter?

JOSEF. I do wish your Highness would not use just that expression. You see, the lady said that if her husband found her here, he would leave over *my* dead body.

PRINCE. I expect he will. So better enjoy yourself while you can.

JOSEF. Yes, your Highness. But how?

PRINCE. Good heavens, man, you don't expect me to act as a correspondence course on *How To Make Love?*

JOSEF. Your Highness is so expert.

PRINCE. Well, you know my methods. The first essential is a specially good supper.

JOSEF. Yes, your Highness.

PRINCE. It is so much easier to make love to women after supper. But perhaps, in your case, it is already "after supper"?

JOSEF. Oh, no, your Highness. Decidedly before supper.

PRINCE. Very well, then. Run across to Sacher's and order a supper—the kind you usually order for me. Charge it to me, of course.

JOSEF. Your Highness is too kind.

PRINCE. And while you're gone I'll entertain the lady.

JOSEF. Pardon me, your Highness, but if I go and order supper——

PRINCE. Well?

JOSEF. Well, won't she think it rather odd behavior in a Prince?

PRINCE. Come, now, hang it all! You aren't suggesting that I should run about fetching food for you?

JOSEF. It would add verisimilitude to the innocent deception.

PRINCE. But all my friends will be at the cafe. How could I explain it to them?

JOSEF. *(Gloomily)* I knew it would be impossible.

(Sighs) Well, there's nothing for it. Let me send her away.

PRINCE. Don't keep on saying "let me send her away." I know—you will simply tell her that you always order the supper on these occasions, because I'm too much of a fool to be trusted.

JOSEF. *(Appalled)* A fool? Your Highness a fool? Oh, I couldn't say that.

PRINCE. Why not? Don't you see, when you said I, you would mean you.

JOSEF. What?

PRINCE. You are I and I am you.

JOSEF. Oh, I see. *I* am a fool?

PRINCE. Exactly.

(During this dialogue the PRINCE has been sitting in C. armchair. JOSEF, meanwhile, has been standing stiffly and respectfully at his side.)

MARIE. *(Off)* Hurray, I've found it! *(This is a modest squeal of excitement at something she has just come across in the book she is reading. At the sound the PRINCE and JOSEF start into sudden activity. PRINCE leaps from chair. JOSEF leaps into settee, so that when MARIE comes in she finds JOSEF lounging on settee and PRINCE standing stiffly beside it. PRINCE hands JOSEF cigarette. Enter MARIE, leaving open library door; comes C. with big book)* Well, that's the funniest library I've ever been in. Talk about hot stuff! You know, the man who wrote this book has got what I call a nasty mind.

JOSEF. *(Rises and crosses to L. of MARIE)* You seem to be enjoying yourself.

MARIE. Yes, I know, but listen. I want to tell you something. Do you know those books are covered in dust? That wouldn't be allowed in my house—— *(JOSEF looks embarrassed. PRINCE coughs and gives him an accusing look.)*

JOSEF. *(Summoning up courage and turning on* PRINCE*)* Dust, Josef? Dust—tut-tut!

MARIE. *(Crosses to* C. JOSEF *drops down* R.C.*)* Somebody ought to go over them well with a damp cloth.

PRINCE. I will damp a cloth and go well over them immediately. *(BELL rings off* R. *in hall.)*

(JOSEF *immediately starts to answer it.* PRINCE *coughs.* JOSEF *stops and returns to sit on edge of* R.C. *table, smoking. He and* PRINCE *exchange an uneasy glance. Business as to who shall answer the bell—ad lib.* MARIE, C., *notices this.)*

MARIE. The front doorbell! (JOSEF *rises from edge of table.)*

PRINCE. Yes, madame. (PRINCE *and* JOSEF *signal to each other and arouse* MARIE'S *suspicions that it is another woman.)*

MARIE. Well, it's somebody calling.

PRINCE. Yes, madame. *(More business as to who shall answer bell.)*

MARIE. *(Sits on arm of* C. *armchair)* Oh, well, I suppose it's time another woman came to fetch her pajamas. There hasn't been one for nearly an hour.

JOSEF. But, dear lady—— Ought one immediately to assume the worst? Josef, who do you think it is?

PRINCE. The postman.

JOSEF. The milkman.

PRINCE. The garbage gentleman.

JOSEF. A book-agent. (JOSEF *and* PRINCE *have repeated these four suggestions thoughtfully, as in the game of Twenty Questions.)*

MARIE. I'm not going to sit here while you two play Twenty Questions. *(Rises)* I suppose you want me to hide again? Very well, you'll find me in the cellar. *(Turns up stage.)*

JOSEF. *(Stops her)* No, no. But wait, please, dear lady, wait. Josef, I have an idea. Why open the door at all?

PRINCE. An excellent scheme, your Highness.

JOSEF. If we keep it shut, they can't get in.

PRINCE. I follow your Highness's reasoning perfectly. *(BELL rings again—three impatient rings.)*

MARIE. My goodness! *Isn't* she impatient!

JOSEF. No. No. Not *she,* dear lady. Do—do let us try to be optimistic.

PRINCE. While we can.

MARIE. Very well, I'll go in here. *(Turns toward the* L. *door.)*

JOSEF. *(Crosses, stops her and takes her up* C.*)* No. No. Don't go into the smoking-room. There's no fire there. Come into the library. You'll find it nice and warm in there. *(The BELL rings five times in quick succession, accompanied by loud KNOCKING on door.)*

MARIE. And if I'm not mistaken, you're going to find it nice and warm in here. *(Exits into library and closing door.* JOSEF *is left up* C. PRINCE *takes a cigar.* BELL *rings again.* PRINCE *lights cigar, takes two puffs, when there is another BELL.)*

PRINCE. *(Curtly)* Why don't you answer the bell?

JOSEF. Who, me?

PRINCE. Of course you.

JOSEF. Yes, but you are I and I am you.

PRINCE. Are you my valet or aren't you?

JOSEF. I don't know. I've almost forgotten. *(BELL rings again.)*

PRINCE. *(Crosses to* C.*)* Will you kindly answer that bell?

JOSEF. No.

PRINCE. What!?

JOSEF. If I may point out to your Highness, your Highness is wearing my livery——

PRINCE. Oh, yes. I see. Very good, your Highness. If it's one of my friends, he'll simply think I've gone crazy. *(Places cigar firmly in mouth and, puffing heavily, crosses to* C. *door.)*
JOSEF. Your Highness's—— (PRINCE *stops at door.)* Cigar!
PRINCE. *(Hands cigar to* JOSEF*)* Damn! *(Exits* C. *to* R. JOSEF *crosses to in front of settee with a cigarette in one hand and a cigar in the other, and puts out cigarette in ashtray. Re-enter* PRINCE. *At* R. *of* C. *doors—announcing)* Baron von Rischenheim.

(Enter BARON. *Very big and coldly angry, with top hat and stick in hand. He remains dignified during scene. Comes to* C. PRINCE *drops to behind* R.C. *chair.)*

BARON. *(To* JOSEF, *as he removes his top hat)* Have I the honor of addressing Prince Haseldorf-Schlobitten? (JOSEF *points hesitatingly to* PRINCE. *To* PRINCE*)* Prince Haseldorf-Schlobitten? (PRINCE *points to* JOSEF. JOSEF *looks in anguish at* PRINCE. PRINCE *shrugs his shoulders, yawns and hurries off* C. *to* R., *waving to* JOSEF. BARON *looks at* JOSEF.*)*
JOSEF. *(Very embarrassed)* Yes—er—good evening. (JOSEF *extends his hand.* BARON *ignores it.* JOSEF, *after letting it flap for a moment, lowers his hand.)*
BARON. *(Stares at him fixedly. He is obviously furiously angry, but preserves a portentous dignified calm)* I should like a word with you, Prince.
JOSEF. Of course—yes—certainly. By all means. *(He looks despairingly over his shoulder as if trying to find the* PRINCE *and get moral support from him. But the* PRINCE *has gone and* JOSEF *turns to the visitor again with a sickly smile)* Er—can I offer you a drink?

BARON. I thank you—no.

JOSEF. A cigar?

BARON. *(His anger overcoming him for a moment, shouts)* No! (JOSEF *waits.* BARON *recovers his self-control)* I have no desire to accept hospitality from you, Prince.

JOSEF. *(Meekly)* Quite. *(A pause.)* Nice evening. *(The* BARON *pays no attention.)* It's snowing—Christmas will soon be here. Real winter weather.

BARON. Please!

JOSEF. Quite. *(There is another pause.)*

BARON. *(Eyes him with silent distaste)* So you are Prince Haseldorf-Schlobitten. *(There is a scorn in his tone which causes* JOSEF *to glance down at his clothes and adjust them slightly with a nervous hand. Still more scornfully)* You!

JOSEF. *(Stung, plucks up a little spirit)* Really, I cannot think to what I owe the pleasure of this visit.

BARON. I will refresh your memory. For some time past, sir, you have been daring to annoy my wife with your importunities——

JOSEF. There must be some mistake. *(He casts an agonized glance toward* C. *door. Gives a nervous laugh.)*

BARON. There is no mistake.

JOSEF. Your wife? I haven't even had the pleasure of your wife's acquaintance. Have you a wife? Dear me, how we shall be laughing about this in a minute or two. *(Laughs feebly, stopping abruptly as he catches the* BARON'S *eye.)*

BARON. *(Advancing a step)* Do you deny you sent her flowers?

JOSEF. Flowers?

BARON. Flowers.

JOSEF. Oh, no. There must be some mistake. I *never* send flowers. Always chocolates.

BARON. You sent my wife flowers. *(Produces card)* This *is* your card, I think?

JOSEF. *(Reaching out for card)* Pardon me—a forgery, I expect.

BARON. *(Crushes card and throws it to the floor)* There!

JOSEF. Quite!

BARON. I warn you, sir—*(Advances quite close and shakes cane angrily at* JOSEF*)*—that this must stop. Do you understand me?

JOSEF. Yes, I think I see what you mean.

BARON. I am glad. Another time you will find me less forbearing. *(Crosses up to door and turns to* JOSEF*)* I wish you good-night, sir. *(Puts hat on.)*

JOSEF. *(Feebly)* Good-night. Good-night. *(Moving up* L.C.*)*

BARON. *(Gives him a last look and turns to go. Just at this moment his eyes fall on* MARIE'S *cloak. He stops. A great spasm of emotion distorts his features. Takes up the cloak in his right hand and advances to* JOSEF *up* C.*)* What's this?

JOSEF. *(Approaching nervously to* C.*)* It—it *looks like* to be a cloak to me.

BARON. How did this cloak come here?

JOSEF. It—it must belong to a visitor. Yes, undoubtedly to a visitor. Surely one is permitted to entertain visitors in one's home—visitors wearing cloaks?

BARON. *(After having smelt the fur collar)* This is my wife's cloak.

JOSEF. *(In agony)* My God, don't say that.

BARON. *(Looking at* R. *door)* She is here.

(MARIE *appears at back* C.)

JOSEF. What an absurd idea! I give you my word of honor——

BARON. Don't lie to me, sir. My wife is here. *(Throws coat on chair at back of table, and crosses to* R. *door.)*

MARIE. *(Has come to* R. *of* C. *armchair)* What is the matter? *(And for a moment the* THREE *hold the picture.)*

JOSEF. *(Aside, to her)* Othello!

BARON. *(In a voice of amazement)* You! *(Advances to below table; takes hat off. He is thoroughly astounded, but* JOSEF *takes his movement forward for one of menace. He stands before* MARIE *with outstretched arms.)*

JOSEF. Stand back, sir! *(The* BARON *is staring at* MARIE *in amazement. Calls)* Josef! *(Enter* PRINCE, *who stands up* C. *To* BARON*)* One more word from you, sir, and I order my valet to eject you. My strong, athletic valet. (PRINCE *crosses up to door, yawning.* JOSEF *sees* PRINCE *and follows up* C. *for protection.)*

MARIE. What does this gentleman want?

JOSEF. He wants *you*.

MARIE. Me? Why?

JOSEF. *(With a sudden wild hope)* Aren't you his wife?

MARIE. Of course I'm not.

JOSEF. O-o-o-o-h!!!

MARIE. *(To* BARON*)* Am I your wife?

BARON. *(Crosses to* R. *of* C. *chair)* No, you are not my wife. *(Laughs.)*

JOSEF. *(Crosses round to below* R.C. *table)* What's he laughing about?

MARIE. I don't know this gentleman.

BARON. Of course not. *(Laughing.)*

JOSEF. Will you stop laughing?

MARIE. *(Quickly)* And you don't know me, do you?

BARON. Certainly not. *(Laughs.)*

MARIE. Never seen me before, have you?

BARON. Never. *(Laughs.)*

MARIE. Then I think you ought to be ashamed of yourself, coming here and creating all this disturbance. You force yourself into the house of a perfect stranger—and bully and shout at him. The least you can do is apologize. *(Moves to* L.*)*

JOSEF. Yes, let's hear you apologize. Whether I am prepared to accept that apology I will tell you later, after consideration.

BARON. *(Crossing to* JOSEF *and smiling)* I am sorry, Prince. I have made a mistake—I will trespass on you no further. I wish you good-night. *(The* BARON *offers his hand.* JOSEF, *about to take it, looks at* PRINCE, *asking silently, "Shall I shake hands with him?" The* PRINCE *shakes his head.* JOSEF *puts his hand behind his back with a flourish.)*

JOSEF. Josef, show the gentleman out. (PRINCE *crosses up into hall.* BARON *looks at* MARIE; *exits laughing.* PRINCE *laughs and follows him.* MARIE *sits on settee.* JOSEF *crosses up after them to hall; calls out)* And ask him what the devil he's laughing about? *(The front door is heard to SLAM.* JOSEF *re-enters from hall and strides about the stage—very fiercely)* The nerve of the fellow! Coming charging in here and shouting and——

MARIE. You see, I told you I never should have come here. I shall be compromised. Already two men have seen me in your apartment.

JOSEF. Only one.

MARIE. Two, counting your servant.

JOSEF. Oh, don't worry about Josef. He's discreet. You can trust him absolutely.

MARIE. Can I? I'm not so sure. He has a funny look in his eye. (PRINCE *re-enters and comes to* L. *of* R.C. *table.)* Well, it's a lucky thing that man wasn't my husband. *(Rises and takes a cigarette and lights it, standing below* L.C. *table.)*

JOSEF. I could have sworn he was your husband, couldn't you, Josef?

PRINCE. No, your Highness. I was quite sure Madame was not the Baroness.

JOSEF. Lucky for him. I was just on the point of setting about the fellow.

MARIE. It looked to me as if he were on the point of setting about you. *(Sits in chair below* L. *door.)*

JOSEF. I beg your pardon?

MARIE. Yes, and he would have done it if I hadn't come out of the library and proved to him that I wasn't his stuffy old wife. You looked frightened to death.

JOSEF. Frightened? I! Nothing of the kind. This is not the first time I've been in a position like this. You know me on these occasions, eh, Josef? (PRINCE *leers at him and crosses up* C.) I don't ask for trouble, but if people want it, they get it.

PRINCE. *(Returning to* R. *of* JOSEF*)* I think the lady would like a little supper, your Highness.

MARIE. Yes, or anything else to change the subject. *(She rises and crosses to* C. *chair, picking up bag.)*

JOSEF. *(Crosses to* R. *of* C. *chair, taking her hand)* Supper? Supper? Of course. How remiss of me. You must be starving.

MARIE. Well, I *could* manage the wing of a chicken.

JOSEF. You *shall* manage the wing of a chicken and any other part of a chicken that amuses you. (MARIE *sits* C.; *prepares to powder face.)* There is an excellent cafe down the street. *(Commandingly. To* PRINCE*)* Josef! Fetch supper. (JOSEF *bends over her.* PRINCE *hits him in back.* JOSEF *starts up.)*

PRINCE. Pardon me, your Highness. *(Whispers)* Aren't you forgetting?

JOSEF. Eh? Oh! Ah! Yes—yes, on second thought—— *(To* MARIE*)* I will fetch the supper.

PRINCE. *(Winking)* Surely your Highness would not so far demean himself? (MARIE *is powdering her face and so does not see this pantomime.)*

JOSEF. Oh. Yes, he would.

PRINCE. It is a little unusual.

JOSEF. No, it isn't. This is a special occasion. *(Bends over her)* I want a supper de luxe.

MARIE. Oh, you're spoiling me.

PRINCE. *(Taps him again and acts in dumb show —prompting)* And I——

JOSEF. *(With an effort)* And you, Josef, are too much of a fool to be trusted. *(Aside, to* PRINCE*)* I beg your pardon, your Highness. (JOSEF *goes up to* C. *door.* PRINCE *walks below* R.C. *table, laughing.)* Josef, set the table. *(Exit* JOSEF *quickly* C. *to* R. PRINCE *indignantly crosses up to* C. *doors, shaking fist after* JOSEF. *Then crosses to table* R.C. *and clears off two dishes.)*

MARIE. *(Looks at* PRINCE*)* All this doesn't seem to have upset you very much.

PRINCE. *(Looks up, inquiringly)* Madame?

MARIE. *(Rises)* I say, all this excitement we've been having appears to have left you quite calm.

PRINCE. *(Gets cloth out of cupboard)* Only outwardly, madame. A good servant never exhibits emotion. *(Puts cloth on table.)*

MARIE. But supposing that man had been my husband, what would you have done?

PRINCE. I would have extended to Madame and his Highness my silent but respectful sympathy. *(Crosses to buffet for cutlery in drawer and takes it out.)*

MARIE. But suppose the man had—murdered him? What would you have done then?

PRINCE. *(Crosses to head of table)* I would have stopped the delivery of the morning papers, madame.

MARIE. *(Rises and places bag on* L.C. *table, crossing around* L. *end to settee)* Well, it's a lucky thing he wasn't my husband.

PRINCE. Yes, madame.

MARIE. He might have been, you know. Husbands do catch their wives out sometimes. *(Places R. cushion on top of L. cushion.)*

PRINCE. Yes, madame. It is one of the few drawbacks of the bachelor life. *(He puts knives and forks on table the wrong way about, and she crosses to head of R.C. table.)*

MARIE. *(Critically)* Josef——

PRINCE. Madame——

MARIE. Aren't you setting those forks all wrong? Surely they should be over this side, shouldn't they? *(Rearranges them at head of table.)*

PRINCE. Madame is perfectly correct. So they should. *(Rearranges cutlery at table)* Madame was saying—?

MARIE. *(After a pause)* Perhaps you don't believe I have a husband?

PRINCE. Why should Madame not have a husband? I know a great number of ladies who have husbands—more or less.

MARIE. Yes, but you don't believe I have. *(Moves to C.)*

PRINCE. I would believe anything of Madame. *(Crosses to buffet for four plates.)*

MARIE. Well, I have. So there! *(Moves to in front of C. armchair, and* PRINCE *roughly puts four plates on table.)* And he's just like the old bird who was in here tearing up the carpet a few moments ago.

PRINCE. Madame has my sympathy. *(Crosses and takes four glasses off buffet.)*

MARIE. *(Sits C.)* And is he jealous of me? My word!

PRINCE. Too bad! *(Puts four glasses on R.C. table.)*

MARIE. He never lets me go out.

PRINCE. He is wise.

MARIE. What do you mean by that?

PRINCE. Wives, madame, are like cigars. They

are never so good if you let them go out. *(Crosses to buffet for champagne glasses and puts them on table.)*

MARIE. *(A pause)* Josef, you're incorrigible. *(Suddenly)* Oo! Champagne glasses!

PRINCE. Yes, madame, his Highness is sure to order champagne.

MARIE. Josef, don't you get a little tired—just standing around waiting and looking at these little suppers of his?

PRINCE. *(Gets napkins and makes them up)* Oh, no, Madame. Some games are as amusing to watch as to play. *(Puts first napkin on R. of table and second napkin at head of table.)*

MARIE. Josef!

PRINCE. Madame?

MARIE. Come here! (PRINCE *crosses to* C.) I want to tell you something. I like you.

PRINCE. Do you, madame?

MARIE. And now that we are alone, I want to tell you something else——

PRINCE. Really, madame——

MARIE. Oh! It's something I wouldn't tell everybody. *(Kneels in* C. *armchair.)*

PRINCE. What is that, madame?

MARIE. Listen! You'll never guess. *(Whispers)* I haven't a husband.

PRINCE. *(Startled)* Madame!

MARIE. And I'm not "Madame."

PRINCE. Not Madame?

MARIE. No. *(Rises and sits on arm of chair facing him)* And what's more, I'm not a lady. My name isn't Marie—it's Mitzie.

PRINCE. Mitzie?

MARIE. I'm Baroness Von Rischenheim's parlour-maid.

PRINCE. What! (MARIE *rises and pushes him backwards.* BOTH *laugh.* MARIE *walks up* L. *and back to armchair, laughing, and drops down on* R. *arm. He, also laughing, crosses and sits on chair below* R. *door.)*

MARIE. Now you see why the Baron was so surprised when I came out of the library—why he laughed——

PRINCE. Yes, yes. Of course. *(Laughing, rises and crosses to* C.*)*

MARIE. And why from the very first I was attracted to *you*.

PRINCE. Attracted to *me?*

MARIE. Oh, Josef, you attracted me strangely.

PRINCE. *(Burlesque servant manner)* I am gratified, madame. I desire to give satisfaction. (BOTH *laugh.*)

MARIE. *(Rises and crosses to him)* Like to like, you see. *(He looks at her, not understanding for a moment.)* I, the maid, and you, the valet. *(Digs him in the ribs with her elbows and crosses up* C.*)*

PRINCE. *(Laughs)* Of course. What is called a natural affinity.

MARIE. Oh, my dear, I can't tell you how pleased I was that neither of you guessed. Fancy both of you thinking me an aristocrat. Oh, my dear! I *must* have been a lady. *(Crosses to below* C. *armchair.)*

PRINCE. *(Coming nearer)* The perfect lady! Even now I can hardly believe——

MARIE. Oh, it's true, all right. *(Kneels in* C. *armchair.* PRINCE *laughs.)* I'm not sure I'm not more pleased at taking you in than at fooling the Prince. *(Drops in armchair—laughing.)*

PRINCE. *(Crosses to in front of settee, laughing)* Why is that?

MARIE. Well, you know what Princes are—chumps, every one of them. My dear, they believe everything you tell them. Now, servants are different. *They're* clever.

PRINCE. You mean, they have the seeing eye?

They can discern the maid's apron beneath the coat of the Baroness?

MARIE. *(Rising)* Oh, Josef, I love the way you talk. You must be almost educated.

PRINCE. *(Sitting on settee and laughing)* And I love the way *you* talk.

MARIE. Oh, you do?

PRINCE. I certainly do.

MARIE. Oh, you old tiddle-winks! *(Jumps into settee on her knees; pushes the* PRINCE *and sits back on* R. *end of settee with feet on seat)* But listen, Josef, you won't give me away, will you?

PRINCE. Of course not.

MARIE. You promise?

PRINCE. Word of honor.

MARIE. You see, we servants must stick together.

PRINCE. Like glue. *(Laughs.)*

MARIE. Oh, you know, it's terribly difficult being a lady, my dear. That time when he kissed me, I wanted to kiss him back.

PRINCE. Really?

MARIE. Honestly, I did—— And the difficulty I had in drawing myself up to my full height and withering him with one glance, you'd never believe.

PRINCE. *(Haughtily)* You found the Prince attractive then?

MARIE. Oh, yes, he's all right. But—a man in his position—my dear—it scares one a bit. Now, with you it's different.

PRINCE. *(Laughs)* Naturally. With me you can let yourself go. No formalities——

MARIE. That's right. None of that awful feeling that you've a hot potato in your mouth and a poker down your back.

PRINCE. You can't get away from it. At heart we're only really happy with our own class.

MARIE. Oh, my dear, you never spoke a truer word. *(They laugh uproariously and in due course, she looks at him and her right hand in his face, pushes him backwards. They continue laughing and as she heads forward, he slaps her back, causing her to drop to the floor. She jumps up and takes a flying leap into his lap)* Oh, Josef, I'll bet you're glad now you came home early, now, aren't you?

PRINCE. I certainly am.

MARIE. What made you come home early?

PRINCE. Premonition.

MARIE. What's that?

PRINCE. I mean, my guardian angel must have whispered to me: "Josef, go home! Because if you don't——" *(Whispers this in a mock solemn voice and* MARIE *when she answers, imitates him.)*

MARIE. —"you'll miss something good!"

PRINCE. That's it. And he was right. You *are* good.

MARIE. Yes, but not too good. *(Lays her head on his shoulder. They look at one another, smiling. Then the* PRINCE *moves abruptly.)*

PRINCE. Come and help me set the table.

MARIE. Oh, don't be stupid! Must we now? *(Rises.)*

PRINCE. Well, in a minute or two. There's plenty of time. *(Takes a cigarette from humidor on table* L.C. *She kneels on settee and he sits by her.)*

MARIE. Oh, my dear, you don't smoke his cigarettes, do you?

PRINCE. I'd like to see him stop me. *(She laughs.)* I believe in keeping employers in their places. I drink his wine, too.

MARIE. You don't?

PRINCE. I do.

MARIE. My dear, *I* use the Baroness's perfume.

PRINCE. Brave girl! I wear his clothes, too.

MARIE. Oh, I wear hers when I know she'll be out for the evening.

PRINCE. What's more, I bathe in his tub, use his

razor and sleep in his bed. (MARIE *laughs.*) Liberty Hall—that's *my* motto. Liberty Hall!——

MARIE. *(Delightedly—giving him a punch)* Well, you *are* a one! (BOTH *are laughing when* JOSEF *rushes in cheerfully—his expression changes as he sees them. He halts* C. PRINCE *hastily throws cigarette away—rises and stands* L., *and* MARIE, *seeing* JOSEF, *turns and reclines on sofa*) Hullo, Prince! Did you get the supper?

JOSEF. *(Crosses to* C.—*uneasily)* It's ordered. It will be here in a moment. I hope that you haven't been bored?

MARIE. Oh, no. I've been having a most amusing conversation with your servant.

JOSEF. Have you? How very—nice.

PRINCE. *(Advances behind settee to* C. *Formally)* I've set the table, your Highness.

JOSEF. *(Tersely, looking at the table)* Yes, I see you have.

MARIE. *(Rises)* Do you mind if I tidy? *(Picks up bag on* L.C. *table and crosses to* C.*)*

JOSEF. Certainly, certainly.

PRINCE. *(Crosses down between* C. *armchair and settee and offers arm)* May I escort Madame?

JOSEF. *(Drags her away)* No! Quite unnecessary.

PRINCE. As your Highness pleases. *(Crosses to* L. *of* C. *doors)* This way, madame. (JOSEF *escorts* MARIE *to door* C.)

MARIE. You know, he's so intelligent. I always think it's so interesting to get the viewpoint of the lower classes, don't you? *(They exit* C. *to* L. PRINCE *remains, laughing.)*

JOSEF. *(Returns* C.*)* Oh! Your Highness, it's too bad.

PRINCE. *(Laughing)* What's the matter now?

JOSEF. Why do you torture me like this?

PRINCE. What have I done?

JOSEF. Your Highness, don't steal her from me.

PRINCE. Don't be a fool. Set that table properly. *(Crosses behind to settee.)*

JOSEF. *(Remembering himself)* I beg your pardon, your Highness—*(Removes plates and napkins and puts them in buffet cupboard and gets out two lace napkins)*—but I saw it with my own eyes as I came into the room. You were carrying on!

PRINCE. Carrying on?

JOSEF. Well, you were just about to carry on. I saw the signs. I felt as if a knife had been thrust through my heart.

PRINCE. Don't make a fuss about nothing.

JOSEF. It wasn't nothing. The air was full of Sex Appeal. *(Places lace napkins on table and tidies cutlery.* PRINCE *sits* C.*)* I could feel it. Oh, your Highness?

PRINCE. Well?

JOSEF. Did you hold her hand? *(Removes six glasses to buffet.)*

PRINCE. *(Laughs)* Certainly not.

JOSEF. Did you Highness kiss her? Did she kiss your Highness?

PRINCE. Well, really, my dear Josef, you don't suppose a lady—a real, genuine aristocrat like that—would allow a valet to kiss her just because she happens to be left alone with him for a couple of minutes?

JOSEF. Your Highness hasn't any idea what ladies will do when you leave her alone with a valet. *(Takes up two special glasses and special decanter —grapejuice)* I could tell you stories that would make your hair stand on end.

PRINCE. You've known of cases?

JOSEF. *(Puts clean glasses and decanter on table)* I could write a book about them. Oh! Your Highness, please don't steal her from me. Think of what it means to me. A society lady, a lady of the highest position condescends to smile upon me. Think of what is implied by that word "Lady"—ancient lineage, haughtiness, temperament, distinction—— Winters on the Riviera and summers in Deauville. *(Folds lace napkins in three and places them on table.)*

PRINCE. Josef, you are letting your romantic heart carry you away. Don't cherish illusions. You're no fool——

JOSEF. Oh, yes, I am! *(Places two clean special plates on table.)*

PRINCE. Well, you're in love. But you are making a great mistake if you think there's really any difference between women.

JOSEF. *(Takes table lamp from sideboard shelf and places it on table)* But there is, your Highness. A woman is only a woman, but a lady is a *lady*. That has always been my secret dream. To love a lady who has her own car, buys all her clothes in Paris, goes riding after breakfast and is untrue to her husband before lunch.

PRINCE. *(Laughs)* I see it's no use arguing with you. All I can say is—good luck. *(Rises.)*

JOSEF. Then your Highness won't steal her from me?

PRINCE. Of course not. What on earth makes you think I should want to?

JOSEF. She's beautiful.

PRINCE. So are a thousand women. *(Strokes* MARIE'S *cloak.)*

JOSEF. And what lovely perfume she uses!

PRINCE. It can be bought anywhere at so much the bottle. But, cheer up, Josef. You may trust me. I made a bargain and I'll stick to it.

JOSEF. *(Crossing to* C.*)* And your Highness really will continue to play the valet?

PRINCE. As long as you continue to play the Prince.

JOSEF. Ah!

PRINCE. By the way, how do you find you get on in that capacity? Everything successful?

JOSEF. Well, yes—and no, your Highness.

PRINCE. You mean you haven't dazzled the lady?

JOSEF. I *think* I have dazzled her, but it's so difficult to make real progress.

PRINCE. I see.

JOSEF. These great society ladies are so aloof, your Highness—so remote—so cold.

PRINCE. She didn't strike me as cold.

JOSEF. It's the—conversation—the little airy nothings that I don't seem able to manage. Now, if I might humbly beg your Highness to write me down a few sentences—— *(Takes a memorandum pad from table and hands it to* PRINCE.*)*

PRINCE. A few tried and true sentences.

JOSEF. Yes, your Highness.

PRINCE. Very well. You want something tolerably burning, I take it?

JOSEF. Extremely burning, your Highness.

PRINCE. Very well. *(Starts to write on pad)* I'll jot you down a few notes and leave them under your plate.

JOSEF. Thank you, your Highness. That will be admirable. I shall feel more princely now. *(Moves towards* R.C. *table.)*

PRINCE. That's good. I'm sorry you're finding the role difficult. Mine has come quite naturally to me. (JOSEF *gives* PRINCE *a look.*) I'm beginning to think Nature intended me for a valet.

JOSEF. Indeed, your Highness? *(Picks up* BARON'S *card from floor, if it is visible.)*

PRINCE. Watch me when I wait on you at supper!

JOSEF. Oh! But your Highness isn't going to wait on us at supper?

PRINCE. Certainly! I'm looking forward to it.

JOSEF. *(Through his teeth)* I am extremely grateful to your Highness. And—er—after supper——?

PRINCE. What happens then?
JOSEF. Your Highness will have to leave us then.
PRINCE. Alone? I understand, Josef.
JOSEF. That, if I may say so, is the crucial moment.
PRINCE. I won't be in the way. I'll go to bed.
JOSEF. Yes, your Highness. But where?
PRINCE. I believe I have a bedroom, have I not?
JOSEF. Not tonight.
PRINCE. What?
JOSEF. If your Highness will recollect your Highness said: "You are I and I are you." So, of course, your Highness certainly can't sleep in your Highness's bedroom, because it isn't your Highness's bedroom, it's *my* bedroom.
PRINCE. *(Replaces pencil in pad)* This is too much.
JOSEF. We must have system.
PRINCE. I'll be damned if I'm going to sleep in your room. *(Puts pad on L.C. table.)*
JOSEF. It's a very nice room, your Highness. Comfortable bed—texts on the walls—— But, of course, if you'd rather not——
PRINCE. You can take it as official that I'd much rather not.
JOSEF. Then perhaps the simplest solution and the one most satisfactory to all parties would be for your Highness to sleep out tonight.
PRINCE. What?
JOSEF. I merely threw it out as a suggestion.
PRINCE. *(Advances) Have* you the nerve to suggest turning me out of my own home?
JOSEF. But, your Highness——
PRINCE. There *are* limits.
JOSEF. I could recommend a most excellent hotel——
PRINCE. Well, of all the——
JOSEF. I have heard The Bristol very well spoken of. (PRINCE *crosses to below table* R.) I think it's

very hard on me. First your Highness shifts the whole affair on to my shoulders—and then you let me down.

PRINCE. Now, listen——

JOSEF. One spends a lifetime yearning for real romance, dreaming of the grand passion—and then the whole thing is wrecked on the rock of the housing problem.

PRINCE. If you will kindly stop soliloquising for a moment, I will offer a suggestion. *(Indicating room L.)* Why not make me up a bed in the smoking room?

JOSEF. Splendid!

PRINCE. Now are you satisfied?

JOSEF. More than satisfied.

PRINCE. Good. Then that's settled.

JOSEF. Yes, your Highness.

PRINCE. Splendid. Everything's settled. *(Moves toward L.)*

JOSEF. Everything—except one small point——

PRINCE. Oh, my God! Have you thought of something else? Well, what is it now?

JOSEF. Your Highness's tail coat.

PRINCE. Now, listen——

JOSEF. But, your Highness, I must dress for supper.

PRINCE. Oh, well, take it, take it! I'm beginning to feel I haven't a thing of my own left.

JOSEF. I am more than grateful, your Highness. *(Crosses to R.—going)* Has it ever occurred to your Highness how fortunately things happen in this world?

PRINCE. It has not. I haven't your sunny nature. (JOSEF *moves toward* R. *door. Advances to* C.) But one last word—(JOSEF *stops and turns towards* PRINCE.)—if you dribble down the front——

JOSEF. Your Highness may rest assured. I will be as careful of them as if I'd paid for them myself.

I only wish I could borrow your Highness's charm of manner as well.

PRINCE. You would if you could think of a way of getting it. *(Exit* JOSEF R. PRINCE *crosses to sideboard and helps himself to ginger.* MARIE *enters* C. *from* L. *They see each other and laugh, and she whispers to* PRINCE.)

MARIE. Where is he?

PRINCE. Dressing.

MARIE. No! *(They laugh again.)*

PRINCE. Yes. Full-dress clothes in your honor.

MARIE. Well, he does do one proud! Doesn't he? Josef, you didn't give me away.

PRINCE. Of course not.

MARIE. *(Takes a bite of the* PRINCE'S *ginger. Approaching table and crossing in front of him. Picks up two forks and plays with them)* Solid silver?

PRINCE. Quite solid.

MARIE. Same where I work. *(Picks up napkin and puts down one fork.)*

PRINCE. Your people rich?

MARIE. Oh, they wallow in it. *(Crosses and sits on bottom* L. *end of table, rubbing a fork with napkin.)*

PRINCE. *(Sits in arm of* C. *armchair facing* MARIE*)* What are they like?

MARIE. Oh, *she's* nice.

PRINCE. Flighty, I suppose?

MARIE. No. Not a bit. But *him!* My word!

PRINCE. Fond of the ladies, eh?

MARIE. Fond of them! He *collects* 'em.

PRINCE. Dear, dear.

MARIE. He couldn't add me to his collection, though.

PRINCE. Did he try?

MARIE. Did he try? I'll tell you about it sometime. Believe me, the man's a sort of Turkish Mormon. *(Wrinkles up her nose and he rises and crosses to her left.)*

PRINCE. I say, do that again.

MARIE. What?

PRINCE. Squiggle your nose up.

MARIE. Like this? *(Wriggles nose.)*

PRINCE. Yes. That's it. *(Comes close to her)* You know, you're a very pretty girl.

MARIE. Do you think so?

PRINCE. *(Pointing off R.)* I do. And I know somebody else who thinks you pretty.

MARIE. *(Jerking thumb)* The Prince? (PRINCE *nods.*) Yes. I'm getting a little worried about that Prince of yours. Something tells me that if I don't get him cooled off a little, sensational things are going to happen around here. And how does one cool off a Prince?

PRINCE. Box his ears.

MARIE. Oh, don't be stupid—then he'd know I wasn't a lady.

PRINCE. H'm—difficult.

MARIE. *(Rises; crosses to his L. and takes arm)* Oh, Josef, isn't there any way a girl can say "no"—without insulting a gentleman?

PRINCE. *(Looks at door R. A thought comes to him)* I know. At first simply say "yes, yes."

MARIE. Yes! Oh, I couldn't say that.

PRINCE. Then, when he starts behaving like a Prince, say "Not before supper. Afterwards."

MARIE. *(Crosses and sits at head of table R.C. Imitating him)* Not before supper. Afterwards. That's a bright idea,—*(Picks up plate and threatens him with it)*—but what happens to me *afterwards?*

PRINCE. Then say, "Oh, no, please! Not *now!* I've just had supper!"

MARIE. *(Laughs)* He couldn't take offence at *that*, could he?

PRINCE. I shouldn't think so. *(Pause.)*

MARIE. Oh, Josef—what a relief! *(Rises and ambles down* L., *saying:)* "Oh, no, please, not now—I've just had supper." *(Sits laughing on table* L.C. *Impulsively)* Oh, I do like you, Josef.

PRINCE. Do you really?

MARIE. Oh, my dear—you've got class. One can see at a glance you've served in the best families all your life.

PRINCE. Can you really? *(Crosses and sits on table on her* R.*)*

MARIE. Oh! And what a relief it is to see a *young*-looking valet!

PRINCE. *(Delighted)* Do you really think I look young?

MARIE. Oh, rather. Well, young compared with the valet where I work. He's got long white whiskers. But we had a very good-looking young fellow three years ago. His name was Franzel.

PRINCE. *(Repeating)* Franzel!

MARIE. But we had to get rid of him. Oh, my dear, the maids——

PRINCE. He put ideas into their heads?

MARIE. He certainly did. Do you know, he was carrying on with the cook and the kitchen-maid at the same time.

PRINCE. No! How very convenient. So little distance to go from one to the other.

MARIE. Oh, Josef! *(Giggles. Suddenly)* Make a date.

PRINCE. When are you free?

MARIE. Next Sunday afternoon.

PRINCE. Give me a ring Saturday.

MARIE. Oh, lovely! What time? In the morning?

PRINCE. About lunch time.

MARIE. That's no good. She'll be home then. Can't you make it earlier?

PRINCE. Round about eleven?

MARIE. Oh, that's lovely.

PRINCE. Do you like the movies?

MARIE. Oh! Yes. Rather. Dark ones. Come on, now. Let's have a drink.

PRINCE. *(Crosses to head of table)* All right, two glasses. *(Picking up decanter)* But wait a moment. Suppose the Prince came in——

MARIE. Forget him. Come on. *(Takes two glasses off table.)*

PRINCE. Two glasses? *(They stand* C. PRINCE *fills glasses from decanter. Replaces decanter on table and takes glass from* MARIE. *They touch glasses)* To our friendship!

MARIE. May it be a fast one!

PRINCE. *(Puts his arm around her waist and they drink)* If I knew you better I'd kiss you. *(Puts his glass on table.)*

MARIE. Well, if you kiss me, you will know me better—— Oh, that's a good one. Come on.

PRINCE. No, really——

MARIE. Oh, come on! *(WARN Curtain.)*

PRINCE. No, really, I can't. *(Makes gesture towards room* R. *and there is much business of dodging the kiss.)*

MARIE. Oh, come on! I'll show you—— *(Laughing, she takes his face between her hands and slowly draws it to hers.)*

JOSEF. *(Enters in full evening dress, cheerfully adjusting a red carnation in his button-hole when suddenly he sees them. Down* R.*)* Oh! My God! (PRINCE *and* MARIE *break apart. She stands frightened.)* You—— You—— You dare! You have the nerve—— You're trying to steal her, after all.

PRINCE. *(Soothingly)* It's quite all right, your Highness.

JOSEF. Quite all right, is it? D'you take me for a fool?

MARIE. But, really it is quite all right. We were simply—*(To* PRINCE*)*—weren't we?

PRINCE. Certainly, we were. *(Crosses down* L.*)*

JOSEF. *(Advancing on* PRINCE*)* You were, were you? Well, listen to me. I know you. I've known you for a long time—you're deceitful, lazy and you steal my cigarettes. You don't dust the books, but you do drink the wine. And what's more, you presume to kiss a lady of the highest social standing who has come to my apartment to take supper with me. (MARIE *crosses to* R.C. *table.* PRINCE *is amused, and smiles.*) A nice reward for all the kindness and consideration. Well, I've had enough. You're a hell of a valet—(PRINCE, *getting annoyed, advances on* JOSEF. MARIE *puts down her glass on sideboard.*)—you can pack your things and get out. (PRINCE *falls back, amazed—rises immediately.* JOSEF *grabs* MARIE'S *hand)* Come on, Marie! *(Drags her off* R.C.*)*

MARIE. *(As she is going)* You're fired.

CURTAIN

ACT THREE

AT RISE: PRINCE *discovered seated* C., *writing in pad; tears out paper; replaces pad on* L.C. *table. He crosses to* R.C. *table and reads from paper:*

PRINCE. "I love you with a burning fervor which threatens to unseat my very reason." Damn good! "You'll find in me a perfect sympathy and a perfect understanding." *(Folds paper in half so that the first half of the word "sympathy" is at the end of the last line of the top half and the second half of the word, viz.: "athy" is at the beginning of the first line of the second half.* PRINCE *places paper thus folded under small plate on the* L. *of* R.C. *table. He crosses, sits on settee and takes up telephone. Into phone)* Give me Twenty-one—seven—twenty-one, please. *(DOORBELL rings.)* Damn! *(He replaces receiver, approaches* C. *door, hesitates and exits* R. *—to re-enter immediately wearing fur coat. Exits* C. *to* R.*)*

(Enter WAITER, C. *from* R., *with basket containing 4 dishes of lobster, pork pie, glazed tongue and roast chicken covered with a white napkin. He is followed by* PRINCE, *who stands up* C. WAITER *places basket on floor* R. *and a little downstage of* PRINCE; *and removing cloth, takes out 2 dishes as he starts to speak.)*

WAITER. Very cold outside tonight, your High-

72

ness. *(As he speaks he shivers and causes dishes to clatter.)*

PRINCE. Well, don't start shivering till you've put down the dishes—*(Points to sideboard R.)*—over there.

WAITER. *(He crosses and puts dishes on sideboard)* If I might take the liberty, I think your Highness is looking remarkably well.

PRINCE. *(As* WAITER *returns to basket)* Thanks. *(Looking at him)* You look about the same.

WAITER. Oh. Your Highness is too kind.

PRINCE. Not at all.

WAITER. *(Taking remaining two dishes to sideboard)* I hope your Highness will find everything satisfactory.

PRINCE. I'm sure I shall.

WAITER. *(Returning, putting napkin over left arm and coming to* PRINCE*)* We always take the greatest pains when it's for your Highness.

PRINCE. Very good of you.

WAITER. And Josef told us that tonight was a very special occasion.

PRINCE. *(Dryly)* He did. Did he?

WAITER. Yes, your Highness, he seemed quite excited about it. Just as if he were going to eat the supper himself.

PRINCE. *(Sardonically)* Ha, ha!

WAITER. I hope we haven't been too long. The chef is always so busy at this time of year. So many of these little suppers.

PRINCE. Indeed. So wintertime is little suppertime, is it?

WAITER. Oh, very much so, your Highness. Oh, very much so. But then, if you come to think of it, so is every other time.

PRINCE. Something in that.

WAITER. Love is never out of season. Not like oysters.

PRINCE. If they're so busy—(PRINCE *sits* C.)—at the cafe, oughtn't you to be getting back?

WAITER. Oh, there's no hurry as far as I am concerned, your Highness.

PRINCE. *(To himself)* Oh, my God!

WAITER. You see I've been told off to serve, your Highness—they won't expect me to come away till everything's satisfactory.

PRINCE. Everything's *quite* satisfactory.

WAITER. It's a funny thing, your Highness, but the proprietress won't trust anyone but me to carry the things when it's for your Highness. Directly Josef came in with the order, I said to myself: "This is where they'll need me." You see, I've been with the firm longer than any of the other waiters——

PRINCE. *(Bored)* Yes?

WAITER. Oh, much longer, your Highness, much longer. It must have been ten years ago that I came to them. I saw their advertisement in the paper, and I said to myself——

PRINCE. Yes, yes, most interesting. But, if you don't mind, I think I'll wait for your autobiography till I can get it in book form.

WAITER. *(Crestfallen)* Very good, your Highness. *(Starts to go and picks up basket.)*

PRINCE. You see, I'm a little busy tonight. Tell me all about it some other time.

WAITER. *(Coming back quickly)* Any time that suits *you*, your Highness.

PRINCE. Oh, my God. Go away.

WAITER. *(Ruffled)* Good-night, your Highness.

PRINCE. Good-night. (WAITER *exits to hall.* PRINCE *rises and crosses to in front of sofa.* WAITER *stops and turns in hall and glares at* PRINCE—*catching* PRINCE'S *eye as the latter turns his head,* WAITER *exits hurriedly* C. *to* R. PRINCE *laughs, picks up phone and sits on sofa)* Hallo! Give me Twenty-one—seven—twenty-one. Please. Is that Twenty-one

—seven—twenty-one? (BARONESS VON REISCHENHEIM *enters* C. *from* R. *to up* C., *where she stands watching the* PRINCE.) May I speak to the Baroness von Reischenheim? (BARONESS *amused—shakes her head*) Not at home. (BARONESS, *smiling again, shakes her head.*) Are you sure she's not at home? (BARONESS *nods.*) I rang up earlier in the evening and she wasn't at home then. (BARONESS *laughs silently.*) Is she ever at home? (BARONESS, *still laughing, nods and moves down a little.*) Well, when will she be at home?

BARONESS. *(Advances to* R. *of* C. *armchair. Smiling)* In about ten minutes.

PRINCE. *(Rises and replaces phone in box)* Good Lord!! *(He recognizes her)* You! I'm dreaming! It can't be you—— It isn't possible—— How did you get in?

BARONESS. Through the door.

PRINCE. Through a closed door. Now I *know* you are just a vision.

BARONESS. The door was open. Left so, I suppose, by the waiter I met on the stairs.

PRINCE. Then I am not dreaming? You are real? *(Advances to her* C. *on her* L.*)* If I come close, you will not vanish?

BARONESS. Not if you don't come *too* close.

PRINCE. *(Advances nearer)* Forgive me if I seem bewildered. For weeks I have been haunting the streets outside your house, hoping that you would glance at me—and now you are actually here, in my own home.

BARONESS. I called to apologize for my husband.

PRINCE. *(Following her)* You mean for having a husband?

BARONESS. Well, at any rate for having a husband who bursts into the house of a perfect stranger and makes a scene.

PRINCE. It was disgraceful of him, wasn't it?

(She looks at him.) Fancy daring to think that *you* would come to the apartment of a strange man.

BARONESS. He shall *pay* for it.

PRINCE. Good.

BARONESS. He shan't have suspected *me*—in vain.

PRINCE. That's the spirit.

BARONESS. And I have *always* been so *true* to *him.*

PRINCE. Ah! We'll start in by correcting that little habit.

BARONESS. Really,—Prince!

PRINCE. I was only thinking that you are too good to be true.

BARONESS. Is that the sort of thing you've been saying to *Mitzie?*

PRINCE. *(Startled—he has forgotten* MARIE*)* Mitzie!

BARONESS. *(Crosses to chair* C. *and* PRINCE *crosses behind to her* R.*)* My parlor-maid. My husband tells me he found her here with you. *(Stopping him)* Oh, I'm not blaming you. She's very pretty. *(Turns away from him)* Well, it's lucky for her she's not *still* here.

PRINCE. *(Embarrassed)* Phew! *(Moves toward* L.*)*

BARONESS. *(Turns to him again)* You don't mean she *is?*

PRINCE. Well—er—in a sense—yes.

BARONESS. Really! And what exactly do you mean by "in a sense"?

PRINCE. Well, the fact is, a rather peculiar situation exists in this house tonight. To put it in a nutshell, tonight I am not myself.

BARONESS. No, you do seem a little upset.

PRINCE. You don't understand. When I say I am not myself, I mean that I am not I, but somebody else. And somebody else is not somebody else but I—— But I shall be I again soon, I hope.

BARONESS. I don't understand one *word* of what

you're saying—but it doesn't matter. I must be going. *(She turns to go.)*

PRINCE. *(Crosses up* C. *to* R. *of her and takes her hand)* No, no, don't go.

BARONESS. Surely you don't expect me to remain and hobnob with my own parlor-maid?

PRINCE. Please.

BARONESS. By the way, are you thinking of keeping her on? Because if so, I *must* tell you one thing about her.

PRINCE. What?

BARONESS. She is *not* a good *ironer.*

PRINCE. *(Deprecatingly)* Oh! *(Puts his hand to his head.)*

BARONESS. She'll *scorch* the handkerchiefs. *(Smiles.)*

PRINCE. Please! I know appearances are against me, but I beg you to believe me when I say that I have no thoughts for any woman but you——

BARONESS. Really?

PRINCE. It's true, I tell you. Why do you suppose I prowled for hours outside your house?

BARONESS. *(Smiling)* Well, Mitzie lives there, you know.

PRINCE. I did not send those roses for Mitzie.

BARONESS. *(Softening)* Those roses—— They were beautiful—— Wasn't it unfortunate that my husband should have found your card pinned to them? Another hour and he would have been off to Paris.

PRINCE. And now, I suppose, he decided to stay at home?

BARONESS. No, he left on the nine-o'clock *train.*

PRINCE. God bless him. *(Crosses and takes her hands)* Then will you grant me one request?

BARONESS. What?

PRINCE. Let us drive to your house——

BARONESS. To *my* house?

PRINCE. Yes. *(During this scene he is trying to take* BARONESS *off.)*

BARONESS. What—*now?*

PRINCE. Yes.

BARONESS. But *why?*

PRINCE. I'll tell you later. *(Lets go of her hands.)*

BARONESS. You want to get rid of me.

PRINCE. No, no, no! We'll come back. And then we'll make up for lost time.

BARONESS. What do you mean by that?

PRINCE. Just a phrase. Just an expression. Do come.

BARONESS. I don't understand.

PRINCE. *(Takes her hand and gets around above her and puts his left arm around her)* You will. When we are in the car, I'll explain everything. *(During this speech he is urging her to* C. *door. She resisting. They exit* C. *to* R. *Door SLAM.)*

(Enter JOSEF *and* MARIE C. *from* L. *They are carrying a basket containing five wine bottles. They set the basket down* C., *she* L. *of it,* JOSEF R.*)*

MARIE. *(Sitting on floor* C.*)* Br-r-r-r! It's cold in that cellar of yours.

JOSEF. *(Stands leaning against the table. Facing her)* Wine cellars are always cold—like a woman's heart.

MARIE. Hullo! What's the matter? Are you still cross?

JOSEF. *(Dignified)* Not cross. Just a little wounded.

MARIE. What about?

JOSEF. Considering what took place just now—

MARIE. Well, what did take place?

JOSEF. Can you ask? Didn't he kiss you under my very nose?

MARIE. *(Sits on arm of* C. *armchair)* No. Under my nose.

JOSEF. Oh!

MARIE. Oh, well, forget about it. *(Kneels)* Look at all those lovely bottles and cheer up. *(Takes a bottle out of basket and waves it about.)*

JOSEF. I *am* looking at them, and they don't cheer me up at all. Why on earth did you have to insist on just this particular brand?

MARIE. But it's Chateau-Creneville—Eighteen Ninety-five—the finest wine there is——

JOSEF. For ten years we've been cherishing this wine. It is practically priceless.

MARIE. Why? Is there so little of it?

JOSEF. Just twenty bottles in the world.

MARIE. Well, after tonight there'll only be fifteen. *(Replaces bottle in basket—looks at the bottles)* Oh, look at them! Don't they seem to sort of smile up at you like dear little babies in their cradle? *(Rocks basket like a cradle.)*

JOSEF. *(Gloomily)* My God, don't do that! You have a pretty fancy! *(Takes basket and puts it up between sideboard and radio cabinet.)*

MARIE. Come along now! Where's the corkscrew? *(Crosses below* R.C. *table and up* R. *to sideboard.)*

JOSEF. I don't know. My man must have mislaid it somewhere.

MARIE. Oh, don't be ridiculous. Where do you keep it? *(Pulling out drawer of sideboard)* Corkscrew! Corkscrew! Corkscrew!

JOSEF. I remember now. It's broken.

MARIE. *(Finding it in drawer)* I've got it! Here it is. He must have had it mended. *(Hands it to him. Comes forward)* Now we can start. *(Gets bottle out of basket and hands it to* JOSEF *and crosses to* R. *of* R.C. *table.)*

JOSEF. *(Aside)* It's murder——

MARIE. You do it—your wrist's stronger than mine. *(Sits R. of table.)*

JOSEF. *(Fusses with corkscrew)* This is the end!

MARIE. *(Encouragingly)* Yes, that's the end. Out she comes!

JOSEF. *(Tugs)* But she doesn't.

MARIE. Oh! You know you are awkward?

JOSEF. Well, what do you expect? My man always attends to this for me.

MARIE. I think it's a pity you ever got rid of that man of yours.

JOSEF. *(Taking advantage of this diversion, puts bottle on table)* Are you going to begin talking about him again?

MARIE. Well, you started it. Gracious, Princes who can't take corks out of bottles ought to be careful how they go about firing their servants. Josef was the brains of this firm—— Here, give it to me. I'll do it.

JOSEF. You seem remarkably interested in Josef. (MARIE *crosses to* C.) First you get upset because he came in! Now you get upset because he's gone out. *(Places top chair L. of table and sits, still trying to draw cork.)*

MARIE. Well, think of my reputation. Suppose he goes about telling everybody I was here tonight.

JOSEF. He wouldn't dream of doing such a thing.

MARIE. How do you know that?

JOSEF. I know *him*.

MARIE. Well, you can't trust servants. *(Sits C.)*

JOSEF. Oh, yes, pardon me, you can. Some servants.

MARIE. What makes you so sure *you* can trust this one?

JOSEF. He is a very special sort of servant.

MARIE. You mean, respectable?

JOSEF. Oh, no, not respectable. Far from it. But thoroughly reliable. *(Places bottle on table.)*

MARIE. Well, if he's such *a wonder*, why did you dismiss him?

JOSEF. For you, Marie. For your sweet sake. And you'll never know what a wrench it was. But when I found you in his arms, it was the end. I saw red—

MARIE. Green, you mean, you jealous old thing. Well, it's a pity.

JOSEF. It was inevitable. This house wasn't big enough for both of us. If I had not sent him away—

MARIE. You would have had to go yourself?

JOSEF. Exactly.

MARIE. How you must love me!

JOSEF. Yes, I do—I love you with a—— *(Looks at paper under plate)* "—I love you with a burning fervor which threatens to unseat my very reason."

MARIE. Such as it is.

JOSEF. You are the first woman who has stopped— *(He again refers surreptitiously to paper)* "You are the first real fulfillment for me of what they call an ideal——"

MARIE. Oh, no, no, no. You see I don't follow you. *(Rises and crosses to R. of L.C. table.)*

JOSEF. Thank heaven you don't. Marie, come here and let me talk to you. Come and sit here beside me. *(She crosses and sits on floor beside him—in this way she cannot see him when he reads the paper.)*

MARIE. Um-hum.

JOSEF. *(Trying to think what to say)* Now let me see—— *(Takes paper and starts reading from it)* "Ask her to stroke your face——"

MARIE. *(Raises her head sharply and looks at him. He hides paper behind his back)* What?

JOSEF. I asked you to stroke my face?

MARIE. Stroke your face?

JOSEF. Yes, that's what it *says*—I mean, that's what I said.

MARIE. Very well. Here we go. *(She strokes his face.)*

JOSEF. *(Reads)* "How wonderful that felt—that gentle touch of your smooth, soft, aristocratic hand——"

MARIE. So glad you liked it.

JOSEF. *(Reads)* "Dear lady, you find in me a perfect simp——"

MARIE. *(Starts up again) What?*

JOSEF. *(Hastily)* "—a perfect sympathy and a—perfect understanding."

MARIE. Go on.

JOSEF. *(Takes another look at the paper and reads glibly)* "I love you. I long to hold you in my arms, to kiss your eyes, your hair, your lips—to whisper in our ear—I love you——"

MARIE. Well—perhaps it could be arranged——

JOSEF. *(About to kiss her)* Dearest——

MARIE. After supper.

JOSEF. What?

MARIE. *(Quoting* PRINCE's *words from Act II)* Yes. Not before supper—afterwards.

JOSEF. *(Reads)* "Do you not sense the magic of this hour?"

MARIE. *(Emphatically)* No.

JOSEF. "Will you not summon me to Paradise?"

MARIE. Not before supper. Afterwards.

JOSEF. *(Reads)* "We will love each other—forever——"

MARIE. After supper. Ooo! I'm hungry. *(Rises; crosses below table to* R. *of it.)*

JOSEF. *(Gives it up)* Oh, my God! *(Bitterly)* Isn't that just like a woman? One pours out one's soul in molten words of passion and all she thinks of is her stomach.

MARIE. *(Picks up bottle)* Oh, now really, Prince, please remember there are ladies present! Besides a young girl must eat, you know. *(Loosens the cork)* There! Why, it was easy! I can't think what you made such a fuss about.

JOSEF. *(In agony)* Oh, my God!

MARIE. Oh, look at my hands! Covered with dust.

JOSEF. Honorable dust from the year Eighteen Ninety-five. *(Bows his head in despair.)*

MARIE. Can I go in here and wash my hands?

JOSEF. *(Leaning on table)* All right. Go on. Nothing matters now. *(Uncorks bottle, leaving corkscrew in it. Buries his face in his hands.* MARIE *opens door* R. *and exits.)*

PRINCE. *(Enters* C. *from* R. *in fur coat and top hat—carries cane)* Josef!

JOSEF. *(At table—starts to his feet, picks up bottle and holds it behind him)* Your Highness!

PRINCE. *(Crosses down* C.*)* Where's the lady?

JOSEF. *(Points to bedroom)* Washing her hands. Oh, your Highness, can you ever forgive me?

PRINCE. What for?

JOSEF. For dismissing you. I assure your Highness no disrespect was intended.

PRINCE. Oh, no. I gathered that from your remarks.

JOSEF. I spoke without thinking. But your Highness knows what love is.

PRINCE. *(Taking off hat)* I do, indeed. *(Hands hat to* JOSEF.*)*

JOSEF. Why didn't we send her away at the start?

PRINCE. It's quite all right, Josef. All in a day's work. I'm not offended. *(Offers his stick.* JOSEF *puts bottle on table and takes stick.)* By the way, am I disturbing you? Have I once more come back too soon?

JOSEF. Not at all, your Highness. I am delighted to see your Highness.

PRINCE. You look as if you were. I hope the sudden joy will not be too much for you——

JOSEF. But I am, really, your Highness. If you only knew how she had been going on because I dismissed your Highness.

PRINCE. *(Crosses well down* C.; *sees bottle)* Hullo! What's this?

JOSEF. This? Oh, that's a bottle, your Highness. Merely a bottle containing wine.

PRINCE. I see. For the supper. *(Crosses to* R.C. *table.* JOSEF *backs above* C. *chair.)* Well, so long as it's not my Chateau-Creneville. (JOSEF *laughs uneasily.* PRINCE *takes up a bottle)* My God, it is! *(Furious—crosses toward* JOSEF*)* Well, of all the—— My Chateau-Creneville—— For *your* supper parties. *(Turns and sees other bottles in basket up* R.; *crosses and lifts up basket)* And upon my soul, all five bottles.

JOSEF. We've only opened one, your Highness.

PRINCE. *(Puts down basket. Comes* C.*)* How many times have I told you—?

JOSEF. Yes, your Highness.

PRINCE. What do you mean—"Yes, your Highness"?

JOSEF. No, your Highness.

PRINCE. How dared you touch that wine?

JOSEF. Well, you see, your Highness, we happened to be in the cellar. I was looking for just an ordinary sort of wine. I knew you would like us to have wine for supper—and she, your Highness, she just made for that Chateau-Creneville as if there wasn't anything else in the cellar.

PRINCE. *(Replacing bottle on table)* You shouldn't have taken her to the cellar.

JOSEF. But I thought it would be so romantic. I've always found that the other sex are peculiarly susceptible in cellars.

PRINCE. How was she?

JOSEF. Most disappointing, your Highness. Only interested in the bottles.

PRINCE. You seem to be having a thoroughly unsatisfactory evening.

JOSEF. Yes, your Highness. I don't seem able to make progress at all.

PRINCE. You must be losing the old skill. I always thought you were such a devil among the girls. *(Comes down R. to below table.)*

JOSEF. Among the *girls*, yes—— But these great society ladies are so different.

PRINCE. You find her unresponsive?

JOSEF. Well, your Highness, she will keep on saying, "Not before supper—afterwards."

PRINCE. H'm! *(Laughs and looks at JOSEF)* Curious. Talking of supper, I promised to wait on you. Do you still want me to? If you'd rather not, say the word and I'll go away.

JOSEF. No, please stay, your Highness. Your presence seems to soothe me somehow—— It gives me a kind of moral support——

PRINCE. Well, you look as though you need it.

JOSEF. *(Takes off PRINCE's coat)* I wonder what's keeping her so long. You don't think she's having a bath in your Highness's tub! *(Places coat, hat and stick on settee.)*

PRINCE. Very likely. You never know what these great society ladies will be up to next. By the way, have you your engagement pad handy?

JOSEF. In my pocket, your Highness.

PRINCE. Give it to me.

JOSEF. In my pocket, your Highness.

PRINCE. Give it to me.

JOSEF. *(Reaches into PRINCE's livery pocket)* In *my* pocket. Allow me.

PRINCE. Make a note that I have an engagement for next Sunday afternoon, to see some dark movies. *(Crosses to front of C. armchair.)*

JOSEF. "Sunday afternoon. Dark movies."

PRINCE. You can have the afternoon off, of course.

JOSEF. Thank you, your Highness. Allow me. *(Returns pad to* PRINCE'S *pocket very quickly, turning so that his back is to* R. *door.)*

MARIE. *(Enters* R.*)* There, that's better. *(Sees* PRINCE, *but approaches* JOSEF *and puts her hands on his shoulders)* Josef!

JOSEF. *(Not quite sure she does not refer to him)* Eh?

MARIE. Ah. Good old Josef. Back again!

JOSEF. *(Still at sea)* What?

PRINCE. Back again.

JOSEF. *(Relieved)* Yes, yes. "Good old Josef back again." I was quite surprised to see the honest fellow.

PRINCE. And his Highness has forgiven me—everything.

MARIE. Splendid.

JOSEF. I have taken him once more into my service.

PRINCE. I cannot express my gratitude to your Highness.

MARIE. And what about me? I'm the one you ought to be grateful to. Really I pleaded for you with the Prince.

PRINCE. Thank you very much, madame.

MARIE. Oh, *I* talked to him. *Well,* now what about supper? Nothing to stop us starting, is there?

PRINCE. Nothing, madame. *(Crosses* R. *below* R.C. *table.* JOSEF *backs up* C. *and takes up the bottle of wine and* MARIE *crosses to* L.*)* May good digestion wait on appetite.

MARIE. *(Noticing* PRINCE *and stopping)* Where are you going with that?

PRINCE. *(Formally)* To ensure the correct temperature, madame, the wine should be placed in hot water.

MARIE. *(Relieved)* Well, you place it back on the table. *(He does so.)* I always get so nervous when I see people taking wine away from me. *(Crosses and starts to sit down R. of table.)*

PRINCE. *(Pushing chair under table.* JOSEF *places* L. *chair at head of table for her)* Pardon me, madame. That is his Highness's chair.

MARIE. Well, aren't you particular. *(Sits at head of table in chair* JOSEF *holds ready for her.* PRINCE *pulls chair* R. *out again for* JOSEF *to sit in, and* PRINCE *pushes in chair, giving* JOSEF *a push.)* Ooo! I'm as hungry as a starving Terra del Fuegan. (PRINCE *fetches a dish and starts to serve* JOSEF.) Josef, Josef! Ladies first!

JOSEF. Certainly. Of course. What are you thinking about, my good man?

(BARONESS *enters quietly* C. *She wears a parlormaid's uniform and apron.)*

PRINCE. It's quite all right, your Highness. *(Catching* BARONESS's *eye)* Madame will get everything that's coming to her. (BARONESS *crosses to* L. *of* MARIE.)

MARIE. I've never enjoyed myself so much.

BARONESS. Can *I* serve Madame? (MARIE *turns, sees* BARONESS *and jumps up with a scream and* JOSEF *rises, staring at* BARONESS.)

MARIE. *(To* BARONESS*)* Oh, my lady—— Oh, my lady—— Oh, my lady. *(Turns away.)*

BARONESS. Quite a surprise for you, eh?

MARIE. Oh, my lady——

JOSEF. Why do you keep saying "My lady"?

PRINCE. *(Moves near to* JOSEF*)* I think it must be because she is this lady's parlor maid.

BARONESS. Yes. My parlor maid, Mitzie.

JOSEF. Mitzie! (BARONESS *crosses to behind* C. *chair.*)

MARIE. Oh, my lady—it was only a little joke. I *hope* you will forgive me. *(Coming down and turning to* JOSEF*)* I hope your Highness will forgive me, too.

JOSEF. Merely Mitzie!

PRINCE. *(Above table)* I think, my dear Josef, the time has come for you to disclose *your* identity.

MARIE. Josef? Aren't you Prince Rudolf?

JOSEF. *(Very upset)* No. I'm Josef. *(Points to* PRINCE.*)*

MARIE. Oh, my lady! Oh, my lady!

JOSEF. *(Indicating* PRINCE*)* His Highness.

MARIE. *(Turns and curtseys to* PRINCE*)* Oh, my lady. Just Josef! *(Crosses up* C., *crying.)*

JOSEF. Merely Mitzie! *(Turns and leans on back of chair* R. *of table.)*

BARONESS. *(Moving a pace to* L.*)* I suppose I ought to be *very angry* with you.

PRINCE. *(Crosses to* C.*)* But you aren't. How can angels be angry? *(Approaches* JOSEF, *while* MARIE *takes apron of* BARONESS *and puts it on herself)* Don't be so miserable, man!

MARIE. *(Confidentially, to* BARONESS *as she removes her apron)* Oh, my lady, I found him such a lovely gentleman, I know you're going to like him.

PRINCE. Come on! (MARIE *crosses up* C. *out of door to put apron on.*)

JOSEF. Oh, your Highness! Merely Mitzie!

PRINCE. Well, what difference does it make?

(WARN Curtain.)

JOSEF. All the difference, your Highness. My beautiful dream is over. Those aristocratic hands—

(MARIE *re-enters with apron on.*)

PRINCE. Aristocratic be damned! Take it from me, Josef, if a woman is the right woman her rank doesn't matter a hang.

MARIE. *(Crosses down to* L. *of* BARONESS*)* My lady, you must get him to show you his books.

PRINCE. And now, Baroness, I think a little supper.

BARONESS. I can only stay *ten* minutes.

PRINCE. Of course, dear lady, only ten minutes. (PRINCE *takes her arm and leads her to table. She sits at head;* PRINCE R. *of it.* MARIE *draws* BARONESS'S *chair out and* JOSEF *the* PRINCE'S. MARIE *and* JOSEF *start to wait at table, offering dishes, etc.*) That'll be all right. Just put the things on the table. We'll wait on ourselves. You can go.

JOSEF. Thank you, your Highness.

BARONESS. That's all right, Mitzie. (BARONESS *signals to* MARIE *that she can go. She curtseys in thanks.*)

JOSEF. Better take the cold chicken, Josef. We can spare it.

JOSEF. Thank you very much, your Highness. *(Takes chicken dish and crosses up* C. *Waiting.* MARIE *steals a bottle and crosses up* C. PRINCE *pours wine into glasses.)* And in case further service is required, your Highness, ring once for the valet——

MARIE. And twice for the maid. (PRINCE *and* BARONESS *smile at each other and clink glasses gently.* JOSEF *holds the chicken and* MARIE *brings the bottle from behind her back and shows it to* JOSEF.)

CURTAIN

"CANDLE-LIGHT"

PROPERTY PLOT

1. Small shelves and on each a white porcelain vase with Chinese lily leaves.
2. 3-corner sideboard with cupboard containing two shelves and drawers and two shelves.
3. Radio.
4. Small shelf and fruit dish and two figures in glass.
5. Small shelf and clay figure, "Lady Godiva."
6. Ornament stand with two half shelves and two shelves.
7. Divan, upholstered brown velvet.
8. Pair brown velvet curtains—rods, rings and fittings.
9. White wood polished table. Rear R. leg wired and fitted with socket to plug in table lamp.
10. White wood armchairs, brown velvet upholstery.
11. Settee.
12. Book shelf table, white wood.
13. 3 White wood dining chairs.
14. 4 Paintings.
    14A Futuristic Woman.
    14B Futuristic Fruit.
    14C Futuristic Canals of Venice.
    14D Futuristic Japanese Fir Tree.

ACT I

On Table R.:
   5 Mats.

2 Plates.
4 Knives.
4 Forks.
On Sideboard, Ready:
2 Decanters (1 containing peach brandy, 1 containing any other liqueur).
Cocktail shaker.
6 Glasses on glass tray.
Dish of eggs.
Dish of ginger.
Dish of almonds.
Dish of caviare.
2 Large glasses.
2 Medium glasses.
2 Small glasses.
On Table L.C.:
Telephone in box (long cord).
Cigarettes in red leather box.
Cigars in red leather box.
Matches in red leather box.
Writing pad (with typed page) in red leather.
Ashtray.
China ornament, "Wild Boar."
Radio Cabinet.
Top and door slightly open.
On Shelves Up L.:
Photo of Queen of Roumania, in red leather frame.
Hand Props:
Notebook (JOSEF).
Handbag and money (MARIE).
Off Stage:
Off R. (JOSEF):
Dress tie.
Off R. (PRINCE):
Dress waistcoat.
Dress coat.
Overcoat.

Gloves.
Hat.
Dinner jacket.
Flowers.
Livery coat.
Pocket-book.
2 Cups of coffee on tray.

ACT II

On Table R.C.:
    2 Plates.
    2 Dishes.
    2 Glasses.
    Decanter.
On Sideboard, Ready:
    4 Plates.
    4 Knives.
    4 Forks.
    2 Serviettes.
    6 Glasses.
    Tablecloth.
    2 Decanters.
    2 Cocktail glasses.
Off Stage Up L.:
    Book (PRINCE).
    Book (MARIE).

ACT III

In Sideboard Drawer:
    Corkscrew.
    Pocketbook (PRINCE).
Off Stage:
    Basket with 4 dishes (WAITER).
    Wine basket with 4 bottles (JOSEF).

HAND PROPERTIES

Cigarette case (PRINCE).

PROPERTY PLOT

Cigarette case (JOSEF).
Cigarette lighter (PRINCE).
Small notebook (PRINCE).
Small notebook (JOSEF).
Coins and bag (MARIE).
Walking stick and cards (BARON).
Bag (LISERL).

WARDROBE

MARIE:
- 1 Evening gown.
- 1 Evening cloak.
- 1 Pair evening shoes.
- 1 Crepe de chine handkerchief.

JOSEF:
- Livery coat in black with yellow dummy and black trousers.
- Waistcoat, gold.
- Tailcoat and trousers.
- White waistcoat.
- 2 White ties (1 made bow and 1 to tie).
- White shirt.
- White collar.
- Dinner jacket.
- Black patent leather shoes.

PRINCE:
- Tail coat, trousers.
- White waistcoat.
- White tie.
- White shirt.
- White collar.
- Black tie.
- Black braces.
- Patent leather shoes.
- Livery coat as for JOSEF.
- Top hat.

PROPERTY PLOT

    Fur coat. (gloves in R. pocket).
    Walking-cane with silver nob.

BARON:
    Evening trousers.
    White tie.
    White shirt.
    White collar.
    White gloves.
    Top hat.
    Fur coat.
    Walking cane with silver nob.

LISERL:
    1 Evening gown.
    1 Evening cloak.
    1 Pair evening shoes.
    1 Evening bag.

BARONESS:
    1 Evening gown.
    1 Evening cloak.
    1 Pair evening shoes.

WAITER:
    Turn-down white collar.
    Ready-made black bow tie.
    Shabby overcoat.
    Black shoes.

CHAUFFEUR:
    Livery great coat.
    Green, yellow collar and brass buttons.
    Livery hat (green with patent peak and yellow cockade).
    Black leather gauntlets.
    Black boots.
    Black leggings
    1 Pair breeches.

"CANDLE-LIGHT"

ELECTRIC PLOT

Foots—2 Circuits light amber and salmon pink.
1st pipe—8 400 W. spots 2 sec. X-ray border 6 light, 200 W. light amber and light pink.
2nd pipe—1 sec. X-ray border 6 light 100 W. light amber.
3rd pipe—1 sec. X-ray border 3 light 100 W. light amber.
Off Stage Left—
    1st Entrance:
        1 strip 160 W. amber.
        1 table lamp on small table.
    Up stage at glass openings—2500 W. bunches, light amber.
Off Stage Right—
    1st Entrance:
        1 strip 160 W. amber.
        2 brackets.
    Up stage at glass openings—2500 W. bunches, light amber.
On Stage—
    Table lamp U.S.L. lit throughout the play.
    Radio set U.S.R.
    Telephone bell in foots L.
    Switch plate L. of C. door.
Radio amp. doorbell and signal light to be placed where wanted.
Base top on R. rear leg of R.C. table for table lamp.

CUE SHEET

ACT I

At rise of Curtain everything out except table lamp on stage and lighting in 1st entrance R.

At cue Mitzie 1st entrance to table, Spot 5 full, Spot 4 ¾ on dim, spot 5 ¼ on dim.

At cue by JOSEF, "Let me show you round the apartment," Spot 5 down to ¼.

At cue everything up full   stands

One 400 W. spot on table R. is used in all scenes at table.

500 W. Bunches on glass panels full up after Radio bring slowly down to ¼.

ACTS II AND III

Everything full up.
All spots full up.

"CANDLE-LIGHT"

MUSIC PLOT

Overture—
   Rosenkavalier
   Weun der Weisse Flieder wieder blut
                          Richard Strauss.
   Hungarian Love Song
   Wiener Volksmusik
                          Karl Kornzek
   Silhouette (O Kaiserstadt, Du schone)
                          Kramer.
   Wien Bci Nacht   Karl Kornzek

Exit
   Weun der Weisse Flieder wieder blut.

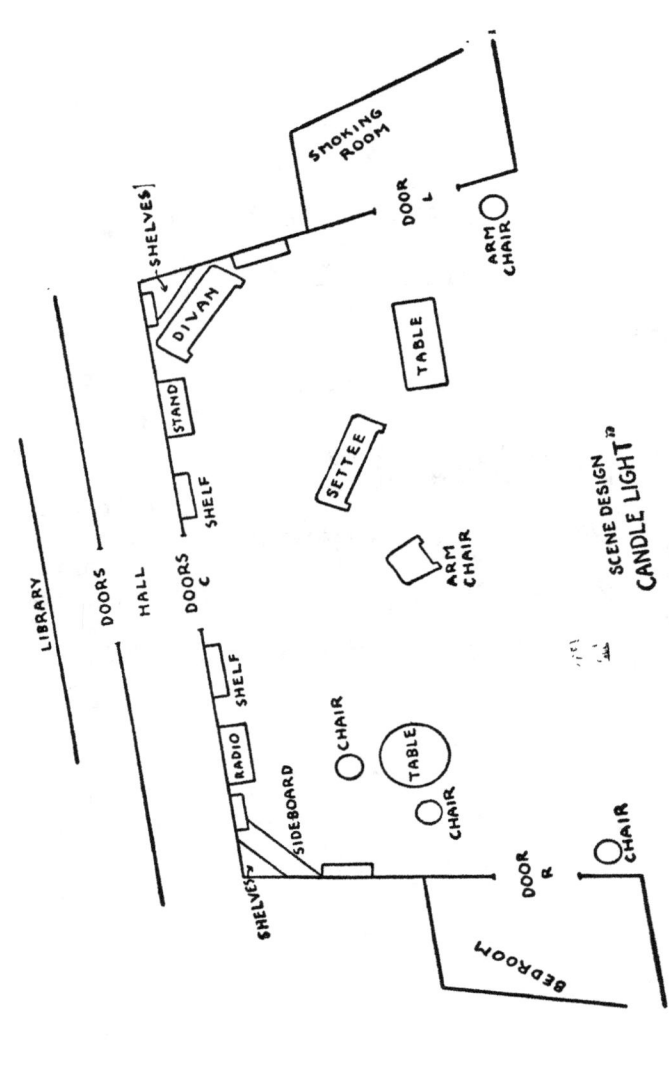

www.ingramcontent.com/pod-product-compliance
Lightning Source LLC
Chambersburg PA
CBHW051407290426
44108CB00015B/2187